"Nothing teaches us valuable life lessons better than real-world stories shared by successful individuals—told with a focus ***not*** on what they have achieved but what they have overcome. I believe that what we learn from adversity is what shapes us and makes us better professionals and people, and eventually defines our legacy. In *Code of Conduct*, Scott Freidheim brilliantly underlines the importance of patience, perseverance, and putting a priority on strong values."

JACK NICKLAUS, the greatest champion in golf history;
individual male athlete of the century, *Sports Illustrated*;
one of the ten greatest athletes of the century, ESPN

"Resilience is hard to explain—hard to teach. When you have read Scott's book you will know."

JERRY GREENWALD, former chairman and CEO, United Airlines

"*Code of Conduct* dramatically shows how we all have ups and downs—but that we are the ones that define our destiny."

MONICA SELES, nine-time major singles tennis champion

"*Code of Conduct* is an exciting story about life and all the twists and turns we face. And that ultimately, success and happiness will be dependent on how we handle the unexpected and whether or not our personal mission is anchored in values. A great read with Scott's personal experiences from which we can all learn."

BILL PEREZ, former CEO, Nike, W

T0272777

"Scott's book is full of challenges—ups and downs in this life. A good balance—performance, sport, endurance, and a strong spirit of freedom explains his success."

WOLFGANG SCHÜSSEL, federal chancellor 2000–2007, Austria

"Scott Freidheim reveals astonishing lessons from a life at the heights of Wall Street to the intimate gatherings of his well-traveled family. The stories are at once death-defying and spiritually uplifting. Take the journey with him, and you'll find values and wisdom in your own life. A great read!"

KAY KOPLOWITZ, founder, chairman, and CEO, USA Networks

"In this highly engaging reflection on his life journey, Scott Freidheim reminds us of the critical importance of reflecting on our values with intentionality and using them to guide the choices we make. To lead a life of meaning and substance, we all need a code of conduct!"

DR. BEVERLY DANIEL TATUM, ninth president of Spelman College; author, *Why Are All the Black Kids Sitting Together in the Cafeteria?*

"Scott Freidheim provides vivid stories from his interesting life to guide us. The examples are sometimes harrowing, sometimes funny, but they are always to the point and illustrate the lessons Scott wants us to heed. Be brave. Be true to oneself. Be moral and care for others. Not bad life lessons for the roller coaster we are all riding."

HENRY BIENEN, president emeritus, Northwestern University

"Scott eloquently describes the importance of an inner score card for life, or 'code of conduct' as he calls it. This is all the more important in today's environment where vanity, likes, and external validation dominate the conversation. Scott's insights are wrapped around with brilliant storytelling, making it a page turner!"

SAMI INKINEN, cofounder and CEO, Virta Health; cofounder, Trulia.com; world record, Ocean Row

"Amazing twists and turns through a well lived (so far) life! And each with an important message about building the core values that are essential to building strong and enduring character."

CAPT. JEFF FRIENT, F-16 fighter pilot (Gulf War), US Air Force

"*Code of Conduct* is frank with a dose of humility. Scott Freidheim shows us that life is hard and the more you level up the harder it gets, so never give up under any circumstances whatsoever. On top of that, we must use unconventional ways of thinking to get through this life and relay our experiences to share gratitude with others and to be thankful for being alive at all."

ALEX FERREIRA, Olympic medalist and X Games champion

"*Code of Conduct* is a captivating first-hand account of how grit, humility, and perseverance can not only get you through life's challenges, but help you come out the other side stronger and more successful."

SARA FAGEN, White House political director, President George W. Bush Administration

"In quantum physics, particles take all possible paths from here to there, the weight of a particular path being proportional to a term we physicists call the *action*. Scott Freidheim makes the case that our own personal weighting function—our code of conduct—is essential for a fulfilling and purposeful life. It is only when the path gets washed away that we see the power of those who have been stepping through life deliberately. *Code of Conduct* is a wild ride through Freidheim's life that you won't want to put down, but when you do, you'll come away wiser to the power of purpose and ready to write your own code of conduct."

DAVE BACON, senior quantum computing physicist, Google

"*Code of Conduct* offers grounded, real-world insights. Scott's principles resonate, and his life experiences are a captivating story. A meaningful read with lessons for everyone."

TREVOR BEZDEK, cofounder and chairman, GoodRx

"*Code of Conduct* is a gripping personal journey of mind-boggling success and power, alongside deeply felt lows. Through it all, there are clear actionable takeaways that are empowering, uplifting, and timeless."

KIRTHIGA REDDY, founder, Facebook India;
partner, Softbank

"*Code of Conduct* is a courageous book by a courageous man. Scott reminds us that the path to success, greatness, and happiness is not a linear progression—sometimes, it's the act of falling that spurs us on to fight our way back up. This humble gift of a book is full of life lessons—a timeless and inspirational book, it is also intensely human and is packed with lessons for us all."

NICK GRAYSTON, CEO, The Warehouse Group

CODE of CONDUCT

SCOTT FREIDHEIM

CODE of CONDUCT

TALES OF THE ROLLER COASTER OF LIFE

Advantage | Books

Published by Advantage, Charleston, South Carolina.
Member of Advantage Media.

ADVANTAGE is a registered trademark, and the Advantage colophon is a trademark of Advantage Media Group, Inc.

Printed in the United States of America.

10 9 8 7 6 5 4 3 2 1

ISBN: 978-1-64225-813-4 (Paperback)
ISBN: 978-1-64225-812-7 (eBook)

Library of Congress Control Number: 2023919722

Cover and layout design by Lance Buckley.

Advantage Media helps busy entrepreneurs, CEOs, and leaders write and publish a book to grow their business and become the authority in their field. Advantage authors comprise an exclusive community of industry professionals, idea-makers, and thought leaders. Do you have a book idea or manuscript for consideration? We would love to hear from you at **AdvantageMedia.com**.

To Alexander, Leopold, and Anastasia.

CONTENTS

INTRODUCTION

LIFE'S A ROLLER COASTER. As for mine, I was

- a CEO for Europe at an investment firm advised by our European Advisory Board members Klaus Schwab (World Economic Forum Founder) and Kofi Annan (United Nations Secretary General). Three years later, I was jobless at home, and my consiglieri was my boxer, Bruno.

- a humiliated fourth string junior varsity soccer player in high school crying to my dad after not playing, yet again, in a game and insisting I was going to quit. Five years later, I broke the all-time goal-scoring record for a National Collegiate Athletic Association's (NCAA) Division I university.

- unemployed trying desperately to come up with a plan. Two years later, we sold the fruits of my vision and our labor (a technology company roll-up) to Manpower for $925 million.

- cycling thirty miles per hour, having climbed 7,000 feet and covered 175 miles in the past forty-eight hours. Minutes later, I was being administered fentanyl on a helicopter that was airlifting me to a trauma center.

- slated to be the next President of a Wall Street investment banking giant with a balance sheet of over a half a trillion dollars. A few months later, the *Wall Street Journal* profiled my house being sold after the company went bankrupt and I had lost my job and was living in a one bedroom in Chicago, on the brink of personal bankruptcy.

- childless to baptizing our first of three gifts from God in the Cathedral of Notre Dame de Paris.

We all have ups and downs—some steep, some gradual—some start high, some start low—and the highs and lows vary greatly for each of us.

Adhering to the principles that we define for ourselves will be the most powerful way to ensure a wonderful, meaningful ride. At times, the pressure to be something we are not will be great.

Today, there is more freedom of choice than ever. That's terrific. However, we need to be mindful of the person we aspire to be as we exercise our freedoms. We don't want to live a free life with little or no behavioral guardrails or introspection to then look back, later in life, and regret not having thought carefully about it in the context of our purpose and legacy in life.

Philosophers, over time, have tried to help us in that.

Religion has been one of the central frameworks throughout history to help followers aspire to behaviors; it certainly is for me. Of course, there has been widespread failure. However, a constant across time and religions has been the concept of the Golden Rule, a principle that you should treat others the way you want to be treated yourself. The Golden Rule appears in virtually all major religions, including Buddhism, Christianity, Hinduism, Islam, Judaism, and Taoism. In today's world, there is a wave of secularization that mutes the standards of behavior that religion provides.

We are exposed to an agenda-driven media and social media that provide visibility to individuals for view count and not role model behavior. We are being deluged with that exposure. At a minimum, it distracts.

Further, corporations manage and filter the information that we see to influence our behaviors to optimize their value, not ours.

How we act and who we want to become should come from within. This is particularly true today as many being celebrated for view count are so for their abhorrent behavior.

Like most everyone, throughout my life there have been countless drafts of personal and professional goals. Yet, it wasn't until face-to-face with death that I wrote down how I aspired to live my life. When falling off the edge of life, in my case, there was unambiguous, distraction-free clarity on what really matters. In my moment of certain death, the only thing that mattered was how I lived my life. The things that were achieved, accomplished, and accumulated were irrelevant. And wow, am I ever grateful to have another chance to improve on the report card for when my life on earth actually ends. What mattered and was important to me was only about how I lived.

My attention span for lessons from the countless individuals with careers like mine has been saturated. However, the edge of life was eye opening enough to me, that it compelled me to share the revelation. To be clear, I am not a role model, nor do I know the right path.

For the most part, we have free will, and we should exercise it for our own agenda.

We have the opportunity to customize the tenets by which we decide to lead our own lives, for ourselves and our families, to avoid a rudderless or manipulated life by creating our own Code of Conduct of sorts as knights had in the Middle Ages.

Knights are well documented as warriors who lived noble lives. History books hail their exemplary standards of bravery, strength, skill, courtesy, honor, and gallantry toward women. That's all great, if true, though a tad heavily overweight on physical combat. But that's history.

Good news is that we have so many modern day heroes in our communities from which to draw inspiration; first responders, care givers, humanitarian aid workers, teachers, medical professionals, spiritual leaders. Their collective code is humbling.

Can a personalized Code of Conduct serve a purpose in the modern world? I think so.

Unlike a millennium ago, there's no chivalric code displayed in a grand banquet room to guide us. The structures that have provided for a personal behavioral GPS are being drowned out in modern-day society.

Living a deliberate life will almost assuredly improve the likelihood that we achieve our desired destination. And that will lead to a life of fulfillment, happiness, purpose, and meaning.

So, I studied my experiences to understand the principles and values that I aspire to and that have contributed to my resilience. I've come up with thirty-two that matter to me and have laid them out in the chapters that follow. They fit within my philosophical and spiritual frameworks.

More than anything, across every tenet that I have defined for myself for the life that I aspire to, it is about willpower in trying to adhere to them.

It's up to you to come up with your own tenets. It's up to you to adhere to them.

I've used personal experiences to bring my tenets to life and introduced them chronologically, for the most part, as I experienced them with an exception. In my life, I have had my share of near-death experiences. So, I'll begin and end with a couple of those moments to highlight the importance of considering creating your own Code of Conduct sooner rather than later.

And while I have failed from time to time at every one I've selected for myself, that does not negate the value of defining a personal Code of Conduct nor the nobility of the pursuit.

C H A P T E R   1

BRAVERY

ON SEPTEMBER 11, 2001, I arrived at my office in New York City around seven o'clock in the morning as usual.

My office was in the World Financial Center complex. Our building was fifty-one stories high, the tallest of the four buildings in the complex, and had over two million square feet of space. It's a building with a pyramid-shaped roof and was connected to the North Tower of the World Trade Center (WTC) by a pedestrian bridge. It is now known as 200 Vesey Street.

We had 5,200 of our colleagues in this building, which we shared with American Express. We also had 618 people in the North Tower of the WTC, 400 people in One World Financial Center and another 1,200 people across the Hudson River at 101 Hudson in Jersey City.

My office had floor-to-ceiling windows and faced south. Directly across from my office was Jim Rosenthal, the firm's head of strategy. To the right of his office was Dick Fuld's office, the chairman and CEO.

At 8:46 a.m., my executive admin Marna Ringel screamed. She ran from her cubicle in the center aisle into Jim's office and put her hands on her mouth. Jim looked at her, looked up at the North Tower of the WTC, and went back to work.

I walked into Jim's office and looked up and saw thick black smoke coming from a very high floor. I glanced at Jim; he had his head down and was working. This was my first observation of how differently people reacted in a new calamitous moment in time. In this moment, whatever DNA created Jim made him just motor on with his strategy work.

I immediately returned to my office, picked up the phone, and called my brother Stephen, who also worked in New York. His assistant told me that he was in his daily morning partners meeting. I told her to get him out. He picked up. I said, "They just bombed the North Tower—it's 100x worse than 1993. I'm outta here."

I put on my suit jacket and walked to the elevator. After pressing the elevator's down button, I thought about our 6,200 employees in the downtown area. Our CEO was at a meeting in midtown Manhattan and not in our offices. I couldn't leave the building. I audibly grunted "F&ck" and made my way back to my office.

To understand my mindset at that moment, let me provide some context. In 1993, I was walking through the WTC underground shortly before terrorists detonated a 1,336 pound urea nitrate hydrogen gas–enhanced device in a truck in the WTC parking garage that killed seven and wounded 1,000. They received funding from one of the terrorists' uncles, Khalid Sheikh Mohammed. I avoided the attack, yet the memories and feelings of the horror of that incident of terrorism in New York City were refreshed in my head.

A couple of our most senior executive management team members were making their way into the chairman's office. I threw my jacket on my assistant's cubicle, knowing that I'd be exiting imminently and walked into our CEO's office. Joe Gregory, the chief administrative officer (CAO) at the time, stood behind the office desk. Our CEO was the most intimidating figure on Wall Street, so any conversation with him better be met with perfect information. Joe looked anxious; he dialed him on the speaker box on the desk and launched into his update.

Paraphrasing, Joe said something like "We think a plane has crashed into the World Trade Center. We are monitoring the situation. We are in touch with the NYPD and the New York Port Authority. We have no additional information. We are monitoring it and will be on top of their direction."

After the very short call, I was perturbed with the interaction that just happened. Wall Street was incredibly hierarchical. Senior folks, as was common practice, dictated the ability of anyone on the team to provide input when it was game time. It was such a developed practice, body language said it all. At this moment in time, Joe was the most senior executive on premise. Unlike at other firms on Wall Street, CAO was the second-highest position in our firm; there was no president or chief operating officer. And on this call, none of us in the room said a word.

As I walked out of the office, I approached Marna. Defiantly, I whispered, "Marna, we just decided not to evacuate. It's the wrong decision. Leave the building now. Walk home. Don't stop anywhere. Do not take the subway. Don't get in an elevator when you get home." She rebutted. "No. I am staying with you until you leave, Scott." To which I mandated, "Marna, you have a choice; you can leave or stay. If you stay, I will fire you. I promise." She saw the seriousness in my words. "Are you serious? You'd actually fire me?" I said, "Yes, I will fire you." She left. It felt great.

My father was in a car on Chicago's toll road with the radio on. The program was interrupted to announce that a plane had flown into the WTC. My father called Jerry Bremmer, president of Kissinger

Associates. Jerry was previously head of counterterrorism with the State Department and subsequently was administrator of Iraq for a year. Jerry didn't know anything but wouldn't rule out terrorism. My dad called me because my office was connected to the North Tower, which concerned him. My dad told me to get out of my building.

To get a better look at what was happening, I took the elevator down to the lobby, proceeded down the escalator onto Vesey Street, walked to the corner of the West Side Highway, and looked up at the North Tower. There was a covered bridge connecting our building with the North Tower. Dozens of people were congregated staring at the top of the WTC, mouths open and shock on their faces. They looked like they were frozen.

Sirens were wailing as New York firefighters who have been known as the bravest of the brave since 1862 were rushing to danger. It was an astonishing sight to see the first of our bravest arrive seemingly undaunted by the towering danger. No foe too big for them.

I walked south along the West Side Highway and under the bridge to get a better perspective. The damage was extraordinary. The building was hemorrhaging black smoke on one of the highest floors. Paper was flying everywhere. Debris was coming down. And when I mean debris, a steel beam the length of a school bus narrowly missed a vehicle that was driving north past the building. I consciously stayed on the west side of the street; the east side was incredibly dangerous. People were streaming out of the North Tower. This was bad. I was there only for a moment and headed back to my office.

Most of the executives who had congregated in the chairman's office were still there. I walked in to join the conversation and relay what was happening on the ground.

At 9:03 a.m., almost immediately after I walked into the room, we heard what sounded like an explosion. We looked up from our floor-to-ceiling windows and saw a burst of flames engulf the upper floors of the South Tower of the WTC. The executive next to me was Jeff Vanderbeek, head of capital markets. He put his hands on his face and burst into tears, the horror crushing his framework of humanity.

Joe re-entered the office. Steve Lessing, head of global sales; Tom Russo, chief legal officer, and Jeff were also in the room. Joe promptly called our CEO. Again paraphrasing: "We think a second plane has crashed into the South Tower. We are in constant communication with the Port Authority, and they are on it. We think we should shelter in place until we get more information. We don't know if it's safe outside." Again, it was a relatively quick back and forth with the rest of us listening keenly. A growing group of our employees was amassing outside the office staring inside wondering what we were deciding.

The message baffled me. Here we were on a beautiful day in September without a cloud in the sky and two planes consecutively hit the two tallest buildings in Lower Manhattan. They were called the World Trade Center towers because they were among the most important symbols of capitalism and had already been attacked previously for what they represented. We had decided to stay put. I appreciated that our CEO was in Midtown and wasn't witness to the scale and graphic horrors of this moment in time.

I scanned the room to find someone else in the room who might also think that staying was a grave and potentially fatal mistake. Tom was formerly managing partner at Cadwalader Wickersham Taft and was our chief legal officer; he was the gray-haired wise man in the room. He had a look of consternation on his face.

The moment Joe hung up the phone, I asked Tom if we could have a word together. We walked to my office. He was often celebrated as one of the top hundred lawyers in America.

"Tom. It's a perfectly clear day. Terrorists attacked the World Trade Center in '93. We know two planes just hit the two towers. What if there's a third plane? What would they hit? We are the next tallest building downtown and we are called the World Financial Center; we are also known as the American Express Tower. We're a possible next target. If we are hit, thousands will die. And we just decided to stay. We have to evacuate everyone now."

Tom immediately agreed. "You need to call Dick." To which I replied, "No, Tom, the reason I asked you to come to my office, away from the others, is because you are the elder statesman, the wise one. You have to make the call."

Calling from the speakerphone in my office, Tom proceeded to lay out the logic. Before Tom could finish, Dick interjected, "Tom, Tom, Tom, get everyone out now. Now!" Tom reminded him of the chain of command and he continued, "Then get everyone in my office now. And I mean now." Within a minute, the same group was on the line with our CEO.

Joe launched into the status of his conversations with the New York Port Authority. Dick interrupted him in similar fashion, "Joe. Joe. I want everyone out now." To which Joe tried to explain the considerations relating to sheltering in place. Our CEO screamed, "Joe! Joe! I want everyone out now. I mean now!"

The mandate to evacuate was launched around 9:15 a.m. I stayed.

Looking down to the street from a window, the street was now getting crowded with more and more brave firefighters, police, and first responder medics. While this was happening, hundreds of New York firefighters were climbing the stairs of the

WTC towers in an effort to save others knowing full well it was likely their last ascent.

September 11, 2001 was a central moment in time in my life. Two tenets of significance to me are inextricably intertwined with the date: Bravery and Gratitude. So I'll continue with my experience on the day in the next chapter. To my mind, we must never forget either.

Never Forget how many wonderful people we have in our community who serve others. *Never Forget* that when firefighters were told to walk into near certain death to try to save us, they went. *Never Forget* how many members of our community have chosen as their life profession, a willingness to protect, serve, and save us if it comes to that. *Never Forget* that, like us, they have families that they want to go home to. *Never Forget* their selflessness and sacrifice. *Never Forget* what bravery means.

When I walk with my three children and we see a firefighter, a police officer, a paramedic, or a war fighter, they shake their hands or hug them and thank them for their service.

The selfless brave earn respect through sacrifice.

C H A P T E R   2

GRATITUDE

A FEW OF US SAT in the chairman's office. Joe had left to execute the evacuation our CEO had just ordered. Twice Jeff Vanderbeek, who was on the couch against the south-facing window, leaned backward to look up at the towers and blurted out, "Oh no, someone's jumping!" "Oh no! There's another one." I couldn't look.

I returned to my office. On the way, I saw a colleague standing at his office door like so many people who were so shocked by the day's events that they looked frozen. "What are we doing?" To which I replied, "We are evacuating." He left.

I forced myself not to focus on the horror. Perhaps, there was an idea or action that wasn't being done that could help someone.

My dad called. He shouted into the phone, "It's a terrorist attack! Get out of the building now!" I said that we had decided to evacuate and that I had to secure a few things before leaving. He told me, "That's a terrible mistake. Get out immediately. Our country is under attack, and you are in the bull's eye." He wished me luck.

Unfortunately, for my dad, the next six hours were the longest of his life as he heard reports on the towers collapsing and estimates of thousands killed. Phone service had stopped. We didn't talk again until nighttime.

I was nervous to be staying in the building. The possibility of a plane hitting our building was very real to me. I relocated to Bill Ahearn's office. He was our head of corporate communications, and he had a television in his office. He had already left, so I sat at his desk and decided to think about what mattered next as most important, now that virtually all employees had been evacuated.

The television was most distracting. News of an attack on the Pentagon broke. My heart sank. When was this carnage going to end? It was crystal clear that we were under attack, and it seemed to me that our building was a logical target (even though I thought erroneously at the time that the Empire State Building was the next most likely target). There was an uninterrupted cadence of attacks ever since the first plane hit. The feeling was one of complete vulnerability and helplessness.

We had to account for all our people—that was next most important—so, I asked Tracy Binkley, a human resources professional who happened to be among the last few people still in the building, for help. She already had started the process with someone on her team. We exchanged our views on the day. I pointed to the burning floors being shown on the television and said, "What worries me is what happens when that fire burns through. Does the building fall to the north, the south, east, or west? It's a quarter of a mile high. If it falls in our direction, we are toast." At the time (because of my lack of any engineering education or experience), I assumed the building would fall to one side, like a tree. Tracy laughed. "You're crazy. They'll never fall." Her confidence didn't give me comfort. It felt like I was straddling a balance of life and death and didn't know which direction the balance was going to tip.

I stayed in the building, in part, thinking I might be able to make a difference. There had to be something more to do to help. My time in the office—for the next thirty minutes—proved most unproductive in that dimension. However, the television was a gateway to soul searching. It portrayed evil, it portrayed bravery, and it portrayed the obligation to be grateful. For me, the televised scenes did even more.

Mother Teresa once said, "A sacrifice to be real must cost, must hurt, and must empty ourselves. Give yourself fully to God. He will use you to accomplish great things on the condition that you believe much more in his love than in your weakness."

Hundreds of first responders were doing just that. Gratitude abounded; yet, retrospection as well. What was my sacrifice? What was my purpose in life? Why did I deserve to make it out? It was soul searching, more than anything, that kept me in the building.

At 9:59 a.m., I was watching NY1, the local station that seemed to have more reporters on the ground than the national channels. The NY1 anchor redirected to a reporter on the West Side Highway. The reporter began his interview; paraphrasing what he said: "We are here in Lower Manhattan with an eyewitness. Ma'am, can you please tell us your name and what you saw?" Shockingly, the camera then focused on Marna, my executive admin, who was the interviewee.

She started something like, "Hi, my name is Marna Ringel. I work at Lehman Brothers. I work on the executive floor. It's a very quiet floor. When the first plane hit, I screamed. I think that threw a lot of people off because it's such a quiet floor. Then … OH MY AAARRRGGGHHH!" Marna screamed mid-sentence on air and seemed to have knocked the cameraman's apparatus to the ground. I wondered. "What now? Why was she screaming? What was she seeing?"

I didn't know if anybody else was still in the building or if everyone had evacuated as instructed by that time.

I heard a voice from down the hall scream, "There's a plane coming in our building—get under a desk!"

On a day when I had heard lots of bad advice, I knew that whoever was hollering was providing more of it and began to sprint to get out of the building. I was a marathon runner at the time and put all my training to work to get out of the building. The building was shaking fiercely. It was terrifying. I wrongly believed a plane was now lodged on one of our upper floors.

As I turned the corner and made my way onto the parquet floor of the elevator bank, my shoes were sliding. The loafers had leather soles that had very little grip on the highly waxed parquet wood floor. Approaching the stairwell, I braked and slid twenty feet toward the door flinging it open.

How strong was our building? When a plane slices through our building's floors, is there anything left to stop the building from collapsing?

We were on the tenth floor. The staircase had a dozen or so stairs that dropped a half floor and then had another dozen stairs that made their way in the opposite direction that together accounted for a full floor.

Starting down the first flight of stairs, I took two steps at a time. My brain kept telling me that there was a plane lodged in a floor above me and that our building wasn't as structurally sound as the 110-story WTC buildings. Our building was going to collapse imminently. I was going too slowly. On the next flight of stairs, I took three at a time. I had to move faster. At the bottom of this flight, I knew that three at a time was too slow as well.

Damn. I blew it! I wasn't going to make it out. I should have left. Mom would be crushed. She would be devastated. I couldn't believe I did this to her.

I thought, "How could I be so stupid as to be the first person to recognize that the answer was to leave the building but the last to leave? I even called my brother within seconds of the first plane attack and told him I was leaving—and now I was going to die for staying too long. I certainly could have left after we got everyone evacuated. I cannot believe this is how it's going to end. I'm such an idiot. My mom is going to be destroyed. Oh, my poor mom. Can she make it through this?"

I had only made it down one floor and concluded that the upper floors were going to collapse. It might have taken seconds. It might have taken minutes. But I was not going to miss getting out by seconds, so I had to move faster. There were roughly a dozen stairs to get down per half floor. The railing was a circular metal piping that made a U-turn at the bottom of each half floor flight of stairs. Trying to jump a full flight of steps would result in me falling at each landing requiring me to then get up and that would take too much time. I elected to jump half the flight (five or six stairs at a time) and focus on landing on a step halfway down the flight and then jumping the rest of the way to the landing upon which, with a light grip on the railing, I would propel myself at the U-turn to launch myself another half flight. I was laser focused on hitting a step after I launched myself in the air each time; there was no muscle memory of taking six or so steps at a time.

The stairwell was empty—not a single person. Virtually all 10,000 or so people in the building, including the American Express employees, were gone by now. I might miss a step and break my ankle, but I figured it was better to try and have to hop the rest of the way in light of the odds of that happening rather than just proceed three steps at a time, which was much slower. I wished I was wearing sneakers. The most important thing was to get down as fast as possible and not miss getting out by a few seconds.

To my amazement, twenty half floors later, I threw open the door onto the upper lobby. I was out of the stairwell. I might get out. I just have to run down the escalator and out the revolving door and get away from our building. My leather-soled loafers had taken me this far. I took a drifting, slippery right turn on the marble floor toward the top of the escalators that led to street level on Vesey Street.

The entrance to 3 World Financial Center had a multistory atrium for an entrance. When entering from the street, there was a large foyer and escalators in front of you that take you to the upper level. I sprinted to the top of the escalators and froze.

The four-story tall windows of the lobby on both the north facing Vesey Street and the east facing the North Tower of the WTC were completely black.

I did not know at that moment that the South Tower had collapsed and that the resulting black smoke was what blocked the view from the windows. I thought that there was a plane lodged in an upper floor of our building and the upper portion of the building must have collapsed and we were now trapped, buried under debris. I froze.

For the first time today, like so many others I had seen become frozen fixtures, I was one of them. My brain was consumed by an unconsciousness of sorts. Acquiescence. Capitulation.

"Run that way!" screamed a fireman standing at the top of the escalator right next to me. It sounded like a muffled yell from somewhere. I didn't even notice that he was there during my slide to the escalator. "Run that way!" he repeated. I had never heard an official, police, firefighter, or otherwise yell. He woke me from my paralysis.

I sprinted west inside the building, thinking about the fireman who was standing his ground. He stayed behind to help others like me as the world was crumbling around him—waiting at death's door simply for the prospect that he might be able to save someone who might still be in the building. As I reengaged into a full-on loafer slippery sprint, the prospect of exiting the building and hope of survival began to creep back into my thinking.

As I was scanning for a stairwell or escalator to get to street level, I couldn't stop thinking of the selflessness and bravery of that fireman. Would he get out? Certainly not. Who was he? What was his name? Did he have a family? Unreal selflessness. Unreal bravery. I had to get out—at a minimum for his sacrifice.

I don't know what escalator or stairs I took (for whatever reason I can't recall at all), but I somehow exited the World Financial Center from the western-most building. I escaped and then distanced myself from the building and made my way toward the Hudson River to walk north by Stuyvesant High School and back onto the West Side Highway. With each step closer to the West Side Highway, the more people there were and the louder the wailing of sirens. The crowds on the street were dense. I was out. It was sunny. The skies were blue. I was out!

I walked up the West Side Highway, stopping intermittently to stare hypnotically in astonishment at the burning North Tower and the deluge of first responders continuing to make their way toward danger. It was astonishing to see how many people sacrifice themselves for others for which we owe a debt of gratitude.

Two people, undoubtedly in the midst of experiencing a horrific death in the inferno, leapt holding hands, falling together.

Why was I spared? What's my life purpose? What's my responsibility now?

At 10:28 a.m., I stood and watched the North Tower sink in a cloud of smoke to a thunderous noise and a chorus of screaming and crying around me.

The North Tower imploded and sliced through my building about ten stories above my floor. My office disappeared from view, engulfed in an eclipse of smoke. The gray cloud of debris was growing and making its way towards me. Was this a bioterror attack as well?

I ran the rest of the five miles from the building up the West Side Highway to meet with our CEO who was in an office on Park Avenue in midtown Manhattan. I stopped in a bar that happened to be open on the way and downed a bottle of Heineken to calm my nerves.

Upon arriving in his office, a TV station focused on a picture of smoke billowing from downtown Manhattan from a distance. It seemed so removed from the graphic and tangible horrors of the site.

We discussed what it was like on site, where we thought we stood in the midst of an unfolding sequence of events and the potential implications.

He decided to have the executive team meet first thing the next morning at our disaster recovery site in Jersey City, a city in New Jersey directly across the Hudson River from our 3 World Financial Center building. He gave me my marching orders. "Put an agenda together."

At the same time, our 7,400 New York/New Jersey–based employees began rebuilding the firm—securing thirty new locations around the city and rebuilding debt and equity trading floors in real time. While our business continuity plans were left behind in binders in the building, the One Firm culture of collaboration that our CEO had established was the real plan. In this moment, he was nothing short of extraordinary.

Later that day when I regained mobile phone connectivity, a friend of mine, Nader Tavakoli, called and said, "Sounds like you had a rough day. Let's grab dinner." That night, we met at an Italian restaurant around the corner from my apartment on Central Park South. The smoke from Ground Zero filled the avenues as the wind was carrying the smoke north, consuming Manhattan. It smelled odd.

Nader asked me if I wanted to talk about the day and how I felt. I quickly replied, completely stressed out, "I don't have time. We lost our building. We don't know where our people are. We have to rebuild the firm, and I have to create the agenda for an Executive Committee meeting first thing tomorrow morning in Jersey City. So if you can help me with that, great." "You're joking," he was flabbergasted. I think he could also tell I had issues.

I scrawled the agenda on a paper napkin. It began "#1. Find our people."

We didn't know at the time, but we lost our colleague Ira Zaslow in the North Tower of the WTC, and fifteen of our employees lost immediate family members. So many lost friends. Everyone was affected.

That night, the first of many sleepless nights, I was hit with a tsunami of paranoia, video mental replay, and panic attacks. I felt very unsafe. The doorman of my building kindly accommodated me that first night when I insisted on inspecting the roof of our apartment building to see if terrorists could parachute onto the roof and breach the building.

That terror is not something that disappears; I live with it to this day. That being said, I was saved. I was out.

My fireman was willingly trading his life for the prospect of getting me out and whoever else might or might not be left in the building. To him. To all firemen, to all first responders, to all community service providers, we owe a debt of gratitude. While all of us may not get saved by one of New York's bravest, we all have someone to thank.

I have tried unsuccessfully to find that firefighter by asking at dozens and dozens of firehouses in New York. Ever since that day, on every September 11, I visit firehouses. For over a decade, I have done it every year with my children. We recount this story to firefighters (some who weren't even born at that time) and thank them. Each time we thank them, I imagine myself thanking that fireman at the escalator. It would be wonderful if publishing this story leads to my finding him so that I can give him thanks.

This year, high school friend Rob Hoff, who now is an executive at Domino's Pizza, orchestrated having over 20,000 pizzas delivered to first responders and thanked them for their service. It is my hope that someday September 11 becomes a national holiday—First Responders Day, to celebrate their service in addition to mourning those that our nation lost.

This year, each pizza box carried a note of gratitude to thank those who serve our community. The note was a September 11 message, but it should be an everyday message.

> Thank you for your dedication and service to our community.
>
> You stand ready around the clock to give your everything to your fellow community members. Most of the community members for which you serve, you have never met.
>
> We rely on you—not every day for all of us—but every day for some of us and every day all of us enjoy the safety for which you provide. We know you will be there when we need it most. If we, or one of our loved ones, are in mortal danger— you will be there and be willing to risk your life to save ours.
>
> You are heroes and role models in respect and civility.
>
> Today is an appropriate day for us to say thank you. On September 11, 2001, 412 first responders died in their efforts to save others. On that day, I was in 3 World Financial Center as the South Tower of the World Trade Center collapsed. I didn't think I'd get out. And after sprinting down the already emptied stairwell, thinking I was too late, upon making it

alone to the normally packed lobby, as the windows were opaque black, I froze. Yet, a firefighter—who was standing his ground just in case someone like me might still be in the building—guided me to safety.

I didn't think I'd get out. I don't know if he got out.

He was you. And I am your community.

We thank you today. You are in our thoughts every day.

God bless you.

Be grateful.

C H A P T E R   3

SUSTAINABILITY

AFTER A DAY OF TRAVEL from São Paulo to a remote location on the Amazon River, an attendant showed me and my brother to our room. He opened the door and flipped on the light bulb dangling from the ceiling. A large tarantula had secured his place on my bed. Grabbing a broom, he shooed it away, saying, "Tudo bem" (All's good). Not particularly credible. I was a tired six-year-old. Not sure where the tarantula went. Not exactly a good night's sleep.

The next day, we traipsed through the Amazon rainforest; it was teeming with life. We went piranha fishing and got exposure to a collection of venomous snakes and constrictors so impressive I still can't shake it a half century later. Try Googling "Amazon jungle snakes" to get the visual—now imagine you're six years old and you are in the middle of them all and see if you get the willies.

When we got back to the floating pile of debris masking as a hotel, we were told there was a swimming pool. We quickly changed into our bathing suits and welcomed a little relaxation. They called it a "natural" swimming pool. The hotel was a floating deck on the Amazon River. The pool was a hole in the deck filled with river water that was 8 meters long by 5 meters wide and 2.5 meters deep. The sides and the bottom of the pool were a steel screen that allowed the passage of water from the river but "not" fish or caimans.

We peered into the "pool" to see a universe of the most frightening, fist-sized floating beetles on the surface of a liquid that was opaque and murky. No piranhas in the pool? "Of course not," we were told. Nobody dared put a toe in the water. We all went back to our eight-legged air-breathing arthropod shared safe space—otherwise billed as hotel rooms.

A couple hours into sleep that night, the lights came on. My dad hollered, "Get up! Time to go crocodile hunting." As it turns out, the black caiman is a species of large crocodilian and, along with the American alligator, is one of the largest members of the family Alligatoridae and order Crocodilian. It is a carnivorous reptile growing to at least 5 meters (16 feet) and possibly up to 6 meters (20 feet) in length, which makes it the third- or fourth-largest reptile in the Neotropical realm. I'm glad the internet didn't exist back then.

My dad was very excited. As we cleared the fog of sleep from our heads, my mom inquired, "Onde estão os salva-vidas?" (Where are the life vests?) Our skinny Amazonian teenage speedo wearing guide (the "Teenage Toothpick") laughed at her question as we boarded a 10-foot-long canoe whose water clearance was about 3 inches above the river and had an electric egg beater for a motor. He warned in Portuguese, "Fall in and the piranhas will probably be the first to get you."

The boat made its way along the riverbank of the Amazon; branches of snake-infested trees combed through our hair. We were plunged into a highlight film of inescapable, relentless creepiness. Only the moon and stars provided light for our nocturnal lunacy. I wondered if the Amazonian tribesmen in the area with their poison blow darts might be watching and unappreciative of our presence.

The Teenage Toothpick stopped steering the electric egg beater and made his way to the bow of the boat. He stood aiming a flashlight on the murky waters. A series of reflections on the riverbank. Each was a pair of eyes. Shining a light across the surface will reveal reddish eye shines dotting the surface because caiman have tapetum lucidum that will reflect light when exposed to light. Caiman everywhere.

He suddenly told everyone to be perfectly silent. As it turns out, one pair of reflecting eyes close by was quite wide, which obviously meant it was big. He quietly navigated us out of harm's way.

By that point, my nine-year-old sister Lynn was crying. She was sitting next to my mom in the back. My mom introduced me to real-time prayer on this canoe ride. She kept repeating the Hail Mary prayer in a steady cadence, on an audible background of tears.

The Teenage Toothpick stood up once again and took his place at the bow of the boat—walking by us carefully to prevent any wobbling that would immediately fill the shallow boat with water. He demanded silence for his performance. He fixed his flashlight beam on a set of reflecting eyes in the water. Then, he leaned into the boat and grabbed a broomstick while keeping the flashlight locked on those eyes. At the end of the broomstick was a small wire noose. He raised the stick above his head and took aim between the eyes of the caiman to lasso the snout. He lunged at the caiman with the stick right between the eyes. Missed! The boat rocked back and forth barely avoiding filling the boat with river water and sinking us all into this evening's American buffet piranha feeding frenzy.

A few minutes later, we were at it again. The Teenage Toothpick raised his flashlight in his left hand and the broomstick in his right. Lunge! "Eu peguei ele. Atenção. Estou trazendo ele no barco!" Say what?! Next thing we knew, he has a caiman whose mouth is clamped shut by the wire on the end of the broomstick and Teenage Toothpick is flinging the caiman into the boat. We all immediately raised our feet as the caiman thrashed about in the barely floating canoe. How the boat didn't capsize is beyond me.

We made it back safely. My dad might not have agreed as he was carpet bombed by my mother with criticism for the lunacy of taking his family on a caiman hunting trip at night on the Amazon under the command of Teenage Toothpick. At the time, the carpet bombing made uncontested sense.

As the years passed, I realized the gift of exposure that my dad has shared with us so generously throughout our upbringing. In this case, sharing with us a piece of the planet that was untouched by the voracious development appetite of humans. We experienced planet Earth in its purest and rawest form that established in me a tangible sample of Earth that we all need to cherish.

Make your presence better for the planet than the one you inherited.

CHAPTER 4

GRACE

I HAD FINISHED TRAINING with our Marymount soccer team in Neuilly-sur-Seine, France, and boarded the #82 bus to go home. I was wearing shorts and a soccer jersey, my legs covered in dried mud.

As we proceeded toward Paris through multiple stops, the bus filled with working men and women on their way home. By the time we were about to cross into the city limits of Paris, just before the Porte Maillot stop, I found myself suddenly in the middle of an existential storm.

A stern and fit woman, perhaps in her early thirties, confronted me in French, saying, "Give me your seat. Can't you read the sign that you must yield your seat to the elderly?" Immediately, I began to stand when at that moment a very elderly man stood up, motioned at me, and yelled, "Asseyez-vous!" I was fluent in French (although anyone of any nationality would have known what he instructed) and sat obediently, saying nothing.

The elderly man was an impassioned World War II survivor who proceeded to deliver a monologue to the entire #82 bus population about the misery in German-occupied France during World War II. He concluded by expressing gratitude for the sacrifices that the

Americans made (I surmised that I was perceived to be a product of the United States due to my ginger hair) to save the French by successfully repelling the Nazis from their country. Graphic details of the suffering of Americans were not excluded.

The thirty-year-old French woman would have none of that. She listened to the pro-America monologue, rebutting strenuously in French, "How can you insult the French resistance?" The combative French woman retorted with a monologue of her own, concluding with, "And they, like this one [gesticulating at me], are savages invading our country."

At that point, virtually every passenger on the bus engaged in the hot debate with a passion as if this was the penultimate session prior to the country adjudicating on how World War II was to be memorialized in history books.

The central confrontation was between the elderly man and the formidable woman. The rest of the bus was a collection of people who were arguing among themselves and poking at the two central figures with their arguments. We were only three decades removed from the end of World War II, so everyone had a firsthand or parental experience that guided their perspective.

My twelve-year-old takeaway was that he was not going to let me stand up or leave the bus without letting me know in no uncertain terms that France was forever appreciative of the support of the United States. His pain at listening to what his fellow citizens were saying about me, a child from the country that liberated him, was palpable.

I sat uncomfortably in the seat closest to the back exit door and considered just jumping off at every exit even if it wasn't my stop. At several points in the melee, I stood up based on the aggressiveness of the crowd, only to have the elderly man yell directly at me, "Asseyez-vous!"

The central French antagonist barked. "Well, what took the Americans so long to get here?" referring to the timing of D-Day, four years after Paris was initially taken by the Nazis.

Thankfully, my stop arrived. I waited until the door was about to shut and jumped off, concerned that I might be followed. The bus moved on; I ran home to the safety of my mother's embrace.

A few weeks later, sitting quietly next to the hors d'oeuvres in the living room of our apartment in Paris in my blazer and tie, I was trying my best not to be noticed for taking more than my fair share of the only ones deemed by my twelve-year-old taste buds as edible.

My parents were hosting a cocktail party; they always included my brother, my sister, and me. The format followed their usual model: a formal affair where a multicultural group of accomplished individuals contributed to the development of a thought, typically social or political, that my father dropped into the room for discussion. My father has an insatiable intellectual curiosity.

At the time, my concern was that the nineteenth-century Haussmannian parquet floors of the apartment were so audibly creaky that I couldn't get up and walk around. As a kid born with ants in his pants, it was incredibly challenging not to be a distracting nuisance in the room. I was oscillating on my uncomfortable antique chair listening episodically to the incomprehensible geopolitical discussion when it suddenly turned real, current, and personal.

One of the guests from Iran was talking about the groundswell of public hatred for the authoritarian monarch, Mohammed Reza Pahlavi, also known as the Shah of Iran. The ideological tension was being fueled by the Grand Ayatollah Ruhollah Khomeini who was living in exile just twenty miles from our apartment in nearby Neauphle-le-Chateau. The public sentiment had triggered anti-government demonstrations that made living in Iran untenable. He referenced bearing historical witness to how quickly things could turn and fled the country in time.

Another one of the guests then queried the group, "How many here have had to flee your home country leaving everything behind?" I didn't realize that was even plausible in this day and age.

Only the two Americans didn't raise their hands. Every other guest was forced to flee their country. I was stunned.

The Lebanese spoke about their ongoing civil war, which had begun a few years earlier. The conflict involved citizen Christians, Sunni Muslims, Shia Muslims, and Lebanese Druze and external influencers from the West and Israel as well as the Palestine Liberation Organization (PLO), Syria, and Russia. "People are fleeing the country at this very moment."

The Palestinian said that he was one of the hundreds of thousands who fled Palestine as a result of the Six-Day War, also known as the 1967 Arab-Israeli War.

The German, who was Jewish, nodded, perhaps not wanting to revisit personal experiences by opening up that door of horror.

The French, also Jewish, who had fled France and returned later, related to the mention of a groundswell of unexpected hatred. She talked about how the French government assisted the German Nazis in both the Occupied Zone and the French-controlled government of Vichy to oppress and, then, exterminate Jews. One-quarter of the Jewish population in France was killed, including almost every Jew that was deported. She talked about hearing of the horrors of Auschwitz where so many French Jews were sent and the multiple times she and her family fled for their lives. "Six million of us were killed." Poignantly, she talked about the furniture and art in their possession at the moment of their first flight from certain death and concluded, "We learned. Only diamonds will save our lives."

The state of our world kept me motionless in my seat. It was a revelation of the prevalent atrocities of recent history and ongoing. How could people do this to each other?

The guests proceeded to have dinner with my parents, and we, three kids, retreated to our playroom for either Pong (a video game) or toggle among the only three available channels: TF1, Antenne 2, and FR3.

After dinner, it wasn't "good night"; rather, my parents made their parental points.

"Thank God you are an American." My father reminded me of the liberties that we enjoyed for which so many had sacrificed for us.

"We should all be thankful. We owe a prayer of Thanksgiving. That we have not suffered as so many others have suffered is a blessing. And we should also pray for those who have and are suffering," my mother reinforced and launched us into prayer. She was always the spiritual foundation of my family.

The struggle for human rights, freedoms, and dignity in our world were introduced to me at an early age with exposure to our frightening reality.

Respect the gift and grace of every human being.

C H A P T E R 5

COMPASSION

IN THE FALL OF 1986, I had just left a party that we hosted at the Psi Upsilon fraternity at Northwestern University. I wasn't drinking at the time as we were in the middle of my senior year soccer season. Driving alone south on Orrington Avenue in Evanston, Illinois, headed toward the local Burger King for my late-night Whopper with cheese, no pickle, no onion with a side of french fries, I saw a woman walking alone. She appeared to be one of the sorority sisters on campus who happened to be walking from the fraternity parties on the north end of campus to the sorority quads on the south end of campus.

Earlier that week, the *Daily Northwestern* newspaper ran a story about a student who had been raped on campus, a revolting violation.

Concerned about her safety, I pulled over and asked the woman if she wanted a ride. She accepted. As an extrovert, I was friendly and willingly chatted. It was a one-mile ride. We drove directly to where she asked to be dropped off. There was no exchange of phone numbers or any flirtation whatsoever. Burger King was next. I never saw or spoke to her again.

As it turned out, her name was Laurie Dann. Prior to my giving her a ride, she had descended into a scary abyss of mental illness. Over the prior decade, she progressed from making threatening phone calls to riding the elevator at night for hours to stuffing raw meat under the cushions of neighboring apartments to ice-picking her former husband in the chest while he slept, missing his heart by one inch and puncturing his lung.

Unknown to me, after giving her a ride, she would talk to the front-desk clerk where she lived on campus about dating me and continued to be fixated on me for the next ten months.

On May 20, 1988, she began her day at five o'clock in the morning making multiple stops with murderous intent. At the home of one family, where she had been a babysitter, she told the parents that she was taking their two young boys to a playdate at a carnival. Among her many stops with them in the car, she took them to a Highland Park elementary school and set fire to the building. On the way home, she passed each of the two boys in the back seat a Mickey Mouse cup filled with arsenic-laced milk and told them to drink it. The boys took one sip and stopped because they thought it was spoiled milk. When she dropped them off at home a couple hours later, she coaxed the family into the basement where she locked them in and set fire to the house. They escaped from a basement window.

On her orchestrated morning, she drove to my house. Nobody was home. She left Rice Krispy treats and Capri Sun packets of juice at the front door along with a handwritten note that said, "To Scott: From Your Little Sisters. Enjoy."

She then made her way to the Hubbard Woods Elementary School where she entered the unlocked doors at 10:25 a.m. She encountered Robert Trossman, a six-year-old boy, in the hallway at a drinking fountain. She dragged him into a bathroom and shot him with her Beretta. Her first shot missed. Her second shot dropped him, hitting him in the chest. Upon exiting the bathroom, she encountered two other boys and attempted to shoot them, but her gun jammed.

She then entered a second-grade classroom with the Beretta and a .357 Magnum. She instructed the teacher to put all the children in a corner of the classroom. Instead of complying, the substitute teacher tried to fight. Laurie broke free and opened fire, hitting five children and killing eight-year-old Nicholas Corwin.

She exited the school and saw a police vehicle that was blocking traffic for a funeral procession. In her panic, she crashed her vehicle. She reloaded her guns, left her vehicle, stripped off her blood-soaked shorts, wrapped a plastic bag around her waist, and ran into a nearby house.

There, she encountered college student Phillip Andrew and his mother in the kitchen. She told them that she had been raped and had shot the assailant. She claimed the police were after her because she had shot the rapist and that it was a misunderstanding.

Phillip negotiated the release of his mother from the house and told her that he would stay with her. As Phillip tried to talk her into handing over her guns, she shot him in the chest. Phillip crawled out the back door to the driveway and collapsed. Paramedics and doctors later saved his life.

She hid in an upstairs bedroom.

A SWAT team surrounded the house. Following a standoff that lasted six hours, she killed herself by shooting herself in the mouth.

Later that day, upon returning home from my job as an entry-level investment banker at John Nuveen & Co in downtown Chicago, my mother erroneously said that sorority sisters from Northwestern left me a care package but that the birds must have eaten it. It was Laurie Dann who had left the items. My dog, Boots, had been vomiting violently. He most assuredly had eaten the Rice Krispy treats she had left. My mother told me that she had placed the remaining Capri Sun packets in the refrigerator.

That night, we watched ABC News Nightline with Ted Koppel as the classroom shooting shocked the nation.

The next morning my mother woke me up, shaking me frantically. She was focused and serious, asking me if I had drunk the Capri Sun juice. I hadn't. She hugged me and told me that an FBI agent was on the phone and wanted to talk to me.

The agent told me that my name was on a list of people that they had found in her apartment and that she had tried to kill everyone on the list. My name was also on a stand-alone slip of paper they found along with a cache of disturbing items. He asked me a barrage of questions.

After the call, I immediately called a former soccer teammate at my fraternity, Wayne Hill, to let him know that she may have left similar items at our fraternity. She had.

FBI evidence technicians arrived at our home shortly thereafter to take the Capri Sun packets. Following testing, they informed me that she used a syringe to inject arsenic in the juice packets. She had baked the Rice Krispy treats with lead.

Laurie had been seeing psychiatrists for many years and had been diagnosed with obsessive compulsive disorder and erotomania, an uncommon delusion that the affected person has a pathological attachment to another person believing that the person is in love with them. An autopsy of Laurie Dann revealed that she had lithium (manic depressant) and Anafranil (antidepressant) in her body. These are drugs that, when taken together, are at times believed to cause violence in patients.

To me, this was about failure, sadness, and tragedy. This was about a woman whose mental illness exploded in destruction at the hands of a system that failed her and ended in her suicide. This was about a child who was robbed of his gift of life. This was about other children and adults who bore the murderous blunt of her illness and suffered immensely. This was about parents and families who were left with a permanent hole in their hearts, lives, and souls.

A lens of compassion
is a powerful companion
in life's journey.

CHAPTER 6

APPRECIATION

ON JUNE 21, 1986, my brother and I enjoyed an historic experience as Brazil and France battled in the Estadio Jalisco in Guadalajara, Mexico, in their quarterfinal World Cup match. The Brazilian side stacked with Zico, Socrates, Josimar, Junior, and Careca had handily won their prior four matches and were favorites to repeat their 1970 victory in Mexico. The French side were European champions with the best midfield in the world led by Michel Platini.

The incredible match was settled on penalty kicks. Pele called it "The match of the century." As we left the stadium, somewhere in the universe our coin of trip fortune/misfortune flipped and misfortune won.

My brother and I had about $1,000 each to our name at the time. We could afford a plane ride, but the trade-off wasn't worth it. Instead, we booked seats on the Tres Estrellas bus line for under $20 round trip from Mexico City. I always liked being in *it*; whatever *it* is in life, you can't understand it unless you are on the ground and in the mix.

The Mexican sun was at its peak afternoon heat. We approached the mob trying to load onto the bus, grateful that we had no bags that were being loaded in the storage underneath the floorboards, as we were able to board quickly and secure two seats. There were clearly more passengers than seats and who knew how that was going to play out. While some of the passengers were soccer fans, the majority were locals—seemingly transporting their worldly possessions, including future meals, in the form of farm life.

The traffic was horrific. Sixty-eight thousand fans somehow all found their way ahead of us on the largely red clay, single-lane, east-bound road from Guadalajara to Mexico City. My brother and I thought we had acquiesced to taking a seven-hour ride—how relatively wonderful that would have been.

The bus seats had a thin plastic coating covering springs that protruded from the weathered material. You felt them poking your undercarriage. Forget about air conditioning; there was no air flow. It was a Mexican experiment in establishing the power of the greenhouse effect. The windows were sealed in the closed position. My brother and I were the only ones who were not chain-smoking Pall Malls to add to the suffocation.

The passengers were restless and loud. The complaints were justifiable. The angry, sweating, shirtless man next to us across the 12-inch aisle decided he had enough of the noise. He reached down into a duffel bag under the seat in front of him and pulled out—a gun? A knife? Nope. He proceeded to remove a car battery, wires, car radio, and detached car subwoofers from under the seat. He then attached the wires and blasted the bus with a static-dominated station. I don't believe he had a volume control for his makeshift audio weaponry. The static radiated through the sweltering heat at the full capacity of the car battery. Of course, I thought he was making a point to get the bus to shut up. Nope. The gods of travel fortune were not shining upon us on June 21, 1986. Rather, for the next twelve hours, he pounded my right ear drum into permanent submission. The next time you say something to me, and I can't hear you, you'll know why: angry, sweating, shirtless, Tres Estrellas.

We crawled along the road somewhere in the single-digit miles per hour. I wondered if I'd make it back to Northwestern for preseason practice at the end of August, three months later. As we made it out of the city of Guadalajara, the red clay road formed a rising cloud of red dust that was sifting up through the floorboards. I watched the cloud rise ever so slowly appreciating that the windows were sealed shut. The red cloud had risen to my knees.

For the next couple of hours, cars passed us, gambling that an oncoming vehicle wasn't coming. The road had limited visibility with turns and hills. Our bus driver, too, rolled the dice with oncoming traffic as he passed dump trucks, cement mixers, and other slower mechanical dinosaurs.

Suddenly, our bus pulled over to the side of the road. Had the bus driver just deliberately saved us from red cloud suffocation? On the one hand, I was relieved that perhaps the stop would settle the red cloud. On the other hand, I saw a slow stream of construction vehicles pass us by that would form a new slow-moving wall between us and Mexico City. Not only were all the death-defying maneuvers to pass them for naught, but we were also going to have to replicate them. I stood up to get the lay of the land only to see another Tres Estrellas bus had crashed.

Our bus driver graciously welcomed their crash victim passengers on our bus. There were no seats available for the balance of the eight or nine hours to come. So, on came bloody passengers and more farm animals. The passengers must have been competing for the Guinness World Record for cigarettes smoked on a bus. Thankfully, I had the window seat as my brother was desperately trying not to get bled on throughout the ride. However bad it may have been to stand for eight or nine hours bleeding next to an angry, sweating, shirtless, chain-smoking, car battery–fueled static blaring man, nothing could have been worse than being one of the people the bus driver had coaxed into riding in the storage space under the floorboards.

When we finally made it back on the road, dozens of dump trucks, cement mixers, and other single-digit-mile-per-hour vehicles had passed us.

The anger and audible restlessness were growing to a crescendo when an unexpected stench cut through the sweltering bus. The onboard toilet was hemorrhaging feces down the aisle. The angry passengers were hollering, their voices competing with the blaring static. The angry, sweating, shirtless, chain-smoking, car battery–fueled static blaring man was getting increasingly agitated, and soon enough, he stood up and was yelling and very angry. He swung his fist at a nearby farm animal and let it be known to all the passengers in the back of the bus that he would not tolerate feces on his feet.

Throughout history, misery seems to require a scapegoat. Fortunately, for the passengers in the back of the Tres Estrellas bus under imminent threat from the angry, sweating, shirtless, chain-smoking, car battery–fueled static blaring man, they secured one in short order. "El Frances!"

There was a non-Spanish-speaking lone French team supporter on the bus who became the target of the Tres Estrella ire. The mob scorned him for having defecated excessively in the bathroom on the bus and causing an intolerable experience for the Tres Estrellas crash victims, existing passengers, and animals alike. They threatened to attack him.

At that moment, I didn't know what his fate entailed. What I did realize was that the mob in the back of the bus successfully established a target should the feces reach the angry, sweating, shirtless, chain-smoking, car battery–fueled static blaring man. He was very angry and very scary. And, fortunately, sitting next to my brother and not me.

Hours and hours later, I appreciated how after twenty-seven years of incarceration, Andy Dufresne played by Tim Robbins in the Shawshank Redemption must have felt after crawling through a mile of sewage pipe and reaching freedom. Just as Andy famously tore off his shirt in the nighttime rain and raised his arms to the sky, so too did my brother and I when we deboarded the Tres Estrellas bus.

While Tres Estrellas literally means three stars, shame on us that we never asked out of how many. Perhaps one thousand? Ten thousand? The only problem, even with those scales, is that it suggests that one or two stars is possible.

I pray for you when it's your turn to meet Saint Peter at the gates of heaven. Because if he turns you away, there isn't an elevator that descends you into the inferno of hell; instead, it's a Tres Estrellas bus that awaits.

Discover our world and appreciate it. Plan for strawberries and cream, but beware of Tres Estrellas.

CHAPTER 7

HUMILITY

ON NOVEMBER 8, 1986, my teammate just passed a through ball ten yards past the offsides trap line of defense as I was running laterally in between defenders at midfield. Turning upfield to chase down the pass, the defenders had to catch me from a standing start. It was a breakaway.

The score was 0–0. It was the last game of my collegiate career. We were playing nationally ranked SIU-Edwardsville led by first team All-American Steve Trittschuh who went on to play in the Olympics and in the World Cup for the US national team.

Sprinting to the ball, I push the ball ten yards ahead of me. The goalie is coming out to cut off the angle. I'm in the clear. Another ten yards of sprinting and pushing the ball ahead again. A defender (assuming it was Trittschuh as he was marking me throughout the game) was about to catch me. One more touch to push the ball ahead another ten yards and steam toward the goal.

Time slows down. Everything begins to move in slow motion. Trittschuh was about to catch me. We are just outside of the penalty box in full sprint. The goalie is perfectly situated eight yards in front of the goal, largely eliminating the opportunity for me to chip it over his head and cutting off the angles to pass the ball into either corner of the goal. As Trittschuh is about to intercept, the cadence of his strides and mine appeared on a jumbotron in my head in slow motion. My objective at this point: get in the penalty box. If he trips me there, it's a penalty kick, and my collegiate track record of scoring on penalty kicks was one shy of flawless.

Knowing that he's going to try to stick his foot out to kick the ball away from my control, I wait until the cadenced time for him to reach me when my stride exposes the ball. Right before that happens, I take a half step to throw my foot in front of his extending leg. He clipped my leg and launched me into the air. To ensure the referee awarded me a penalty kick, it was essential to twist slightly in the air and land on the ball on my ribcage. The referee whistle blew. Penalty kick.

I am standing one on one with the goalie, the ball placed twelve yards from him standing on the goal line, and my penalty kick routine, which was developed by adapting counsel from a sports psychologist, goes into autopilot. A few deep breaths staring at the ball to calm my body. The referee signals for the kick to be taken. Lift the head and visualize walking up to the ball and firmly place a kick in the lower-left corner, one foot from the post. If the ball in my visualization goes in, take the shot. In my visualization, it's a miss as the ball hits the post in my mind. Regroup and start over as is the predetermined routine. Visualize walking up to the ball and firmly place a kick in the lower-right corner, one foot from the post. In my visualization, it's a miss and the goalie saves it. This had never happened before.

The referee yells at me to take the penalty kick. Approaching the ball, having made no decision on shot placement for the first time, I go hard left but make the mistake of leaning back which elevates the trajectory of the ball. The goalie guesses correctly and dives to the left. Luckily, the shot lodges into the upper-left corner of the goal.

Northwestern 1–SIU-Edwardsville 0.

I first played soccer on the burnt orange clay playgrounds of the Associação Escola Graduada de São Paulo. We played before school, during lunch break, sometimes at recess, and after school. In fourth through eighth grades, we did the same in France. In every one of the eleven years leading up to my senior year in high school, with only one exception, I failed to make the team and was cut.

My brother weighed in anticipating my battle to try to make the New Trier High School varsity soccer team my senior year. "Be the guy in the best shape. Win the mile and two-mile preseason races. Be the hardest worker in all the wind sprints. They'll have to put you on the team. The hardest worker always makes the team."

Making the team was a relief. We had a great run before bowing to Granite City South 2–1 in the Illinois State Finals. At Northwestern University, I broke the program's all-time goal-scoring record midway through my senior year. However, in my first foray into a tiny bit of success, my behavior was my worst.

Before each game, I played Billy Idol to get myself fired up. Playing NCAA Division 1 soccer in the Big Ten Conference at 5'9" and 160 pounds, I was always at a significant physical disadvantage. Channeling all the aggressiveness possible to deliver goals on the field, I racked up more yellow cards than the rest of our team combined.

Against the University of Notre Dame, I pushed off two defenders and scored on the holy grounds by punching the ball into the goal with my fist (an illegal move) while feigning a head ball. I stepped on the face of a University of Illinois player who fouled me in the penalty box, sending him off in an ambulance. I spat in the face of a Northern Illinois University opponent. When a referee called me offsides when playing against the University of Minnesota, I stopped in my tracks, flipped the ball up with my foot, and volleyed it at the referee, narrowly missing him.

Overcoming a lifetime of soccer disappointment, I boasted.

I'm ashamed of all of that.

Success on the back of years of self-perceived failure is tricky to manage. In my professional life, I witnessed scores of college nerds achieve overnight social success due to their highly compensated positions and attractive career potential. For so many of them, it was difficult to manage. Many got fired from their companies for their atrocious and loathsome behavior, including several who ended up in the news for the audacity of their actions. Many others went on to great success but were never able to jettison their obnoxiousness.

I'd like to have a redo to be a better collegiate athlete to my teammates, to my opponents, to the referees, and all those I touched. However, I am most grateful for the opportunity to have been able to reflect on it before starting my professional career.

The people we admire the most are humble. They make a difference in their family; they make a difference in their community; they make a difference in their profession; they make a difference in the world. They have the confidence to let their actions and contributions suffice for their own personal satisfaction.

As Saint Augustine said,
"Humility is the foundation
of all other virtues."

C H A P T E R 8

EQUITY

ON NOVEMBER 13, 2006, I sat in the rain with politicians, civil rights leaders, and others gathered along the northeast edge of the Tidal Basin in Washington, District of Columbia, for the groundbreaking of the Martin Luther King Jr. National Memorial. I was part of the inaugural group of donors and attended. The miserable weather didn't dampen the shining moment. President George W. Bush captured a big piece of the significance saying,

> The King Memorial will span a piece of ground between the Jefferson and Lincoln memorials and by its presence in this place, it will unite the men who declared the promise and defended the promise of America, with the man who redeemed the promise of America.

I listened to many reflections on the history of our nation. I reflected on my own. Fifteen years earlier, in September 1991, I was assigned my first project on Wall Street, a convertible bond pitch for Mark IV Industries. I had just finished at Northwestern's Kellogg

School of Business and was a first-year associate. Since it was my first assignment, I felt like if I blew it in any way, I would be out.

Working on Wall Street was a pressure cooker and had a harsh system of weeding people out throughout the career pyramid. As I plugged away on the presentation over the weekend in the office, I heard someone calling. Since I was one of the only people on the floor, I made my way toward the yelling. As I got closer, I realized it was the senior vice president on the project I was working on, hollering, "Lampshade, lampshade, lampshade," in a funny accent. (I realized later it was meant to sound German.) I poked my head in his office and asked supportively, "Can I help with anything?" He continued, looking me straight in the eyes. What he proceeded to explain was the meaning behind his calling was the most offensive thing I had heard in my life. It's too offensive to print. I lost the blood flow in my face and felt sick to my stomach.

I also felt like this was a moment when what I said next could end my career.

Growing up in Paris, I was exposed to the horrors of the Holocaust. We knew Jews who had escaped concentration camps; we met French who were part of the French resistance; we met Americans who had fought in World War II.

"That makes me feel reeeaaalllyyy uncomfortable." Without waiting for a reply, I walked out of his office and returned to mine not knowing what my professional fate would be. He never brought it up again, nor did I. Today, fortunately, corporate America has made enough progress that I could have reported it and continued with my career, and his career would have justifiably ended abruptly. But back then? Absolutely not.

A few years later in 1994, I was dual tasking as an associate in investment banking and as one of two associates selected to run the

MBA graduate school recruiting program along with two managing directors. We had just finished final-round interviews at our office on South LaSalle Street in Chicago. The four of us and the full-time recruiting team (for administrative support) were at the decision-making table.

For each candidate, the four of us would rate the candidate from 1 to 5. When it was time to rate one of the top candidates from the University of Chicago Business School, we went around ascribing to her a rating as we did all candidates. When it was the turn of one of the managing directors, he said "3M." We looked at each other befuddled. The other managing director broke the silence. "3M? Enlighten us." To which he replied with a sound effect "Mmm, mmm, mmm." I almost fell off my chair in disbelief. Nobody said anything.

Later in 1994, I was summoned to this managing director's office. When I came, he looked at me very quizzically and asked, "I understand you support Jim." By way of background, Jim was the most qualified candidate from the Stanford Graduate School of Business. "Yeah." He shifted his head and peered into me incredulously wondering how it was plausible that he had misjudged me. "But he's black," he said. Once again, I had one of those "my career is about to end if I say the wrong thing moments" and blurted, "Yeah, and he's got a 4.0 GPA, a 700 on the GMAT, and an offer in hand from Morgan Stanley. Anything else?" He continued to stare at me for five seconds—it felt like hours. It was unbelievably uncomfortable. "No, that's all." I left.

I, for one, having witnessed anti-semitism, misogyny, and racism firsthand in work in the workplace (and lots more than the three disgusting vignettes) set out to making a positive difference as a cornerstone of what defined me as a professional once I was in a position of authority and could do something about it. While there are so many opportunities to make a positive difference, here are a few of the ones we implemented.

Addressing unconscious bias. For the most part, people do not intend to be biased when they recruit and interview—but it happens. Think of the first five to ten minutes of pleasantries before the relevant interviewing starts. It is much more likely for someone to connect with a candidate if they have shared points of connection like neighborhoods, schools, interests, or prior work experience. These all create common ground that has little to do with qualifications but clearly advantages those who have similar experiences with the interviewer.

I spent time reading the works and meeting with Harvard Department of Psychology professor Mahzarin Banaji, who has studied and written extensively about unconscious bias. Based on learnings from her, we ran a pilot at our Wall Street firm for recruiting students from Columbia University, setting up two teams. One team picked résumés and interviewed the traditional way. The other team adopted a very different process, which largely eliminated unconscious bias. Both teams sent their top picks to the final round of interviewing. The team with the new process had a more qualified group of finalists, and their candidates received more full-time employment offers. In fact, the top-rated candidate from Columbia University was eliminated by the traditional process team during résumé screening.

If corporate America invested the time to create hiring programs that addressed unconscious bias, they'd enjoy a more talented employee base, and we'd all benefit from a more competitive economy.

Another, helping level the opportunity playing field. Some companies require diverse candidate slates in the interviewing process; that is easily implemented and good. We implemented the no-cost directive everywhere I worked. However, much more can be done by corporate America to level the playing field.

When I worked on Wall Street, we established a mentorship program with Spelman College, an all-female HBCU (Historically

Black Colleges and Universities). We assigned vice presidents at our firm one Spelman undergraduate student to mentor and established that 10 percent of each of the vice presidents' bonus would be zeroed out or potentially quadrupled based on where their mentee ended up professionally after graduation. That created an economic incentive for the Wall Street insiders to use their insights and networks to benefit the women of Spelman, including what careers they should pursue, how to approach a company, making introductions, and training on how to interview. By establishing this process, some socioeconomic-dependent privileges are leveled, and many more qualified students make it to and through the hiring process. Mentorship backed by economic incentive can work.

Diversity and inclusion efforts are too often implemented as marketing and branding, legal protection, and philanthropy. Diversity and inclusion shouldn't be a cost of doing business. It should be good business.

Working on Wall Street, on my watch, we increased the number of Black people in investment banking and capital markets (the most highly compensated positions at the firm) by a factor of ten while improving candidate qualifications through these and other initiatives.

This year, I revisited the Martin Luther King Jr. National Memorial with my three children and read to them his words on the monument: "Out of the mountain of despair, a stone of hope."

The land of opportunity rests on our commitment to it.

CHAPTER 9

RISK

I HAD JUST FINISHED SPEAKING on a panel about innovation at the World Economic Forum's (WEF) annual meeting in Davos, Switzerland. This particular gathering was one of the closed-door sessions except for the most prominent CEOs from the technology, media, and telecommunications (TMT) industries—the WEF calls these Governors' Meetings. I was there as a panelist with Mike Fries, CEO of Liberty Global. Invited panelists, who were not part of the invited industry CEOs, came only for their panel and left.

There were roughly forty CEOs in the room. Every comment I made was so carefully researched and rehearsed, I was largely on autopilot on stage. Immediately following the end of our session, there was a ten-minute break before the group embarked on their next session. That's the window I got to try to create business opportunities before I had to leave. There were no other investment bankers in the room, so it was a rare, great environment.

Best I could surmise, all the expected CEOs in the room with whom we wanted to do business with were in the room with one exception, a twenty-three-year-old named Mark Zuckerberg. He wasn't on our list of anticipated attendees. My team had researched the attendee list weeks in advance and provided me with briefings and talking points to deliver to each CEO to communicate productively with as many as possible.

Mark had founded Facebook three years earlier and already had fifteen million users. It was a private company that was experiencing meteoric growth, even if it made little money.

I decided to allocate all my time with Mark at the expense of my opportunity with all others. He looked like he was in high school and dressed the part.

My pitch to him was Facebook going public. I laid out the benefits and considerations.

It was difficult to get any feedback cues. While he had already built quite a specific personality-type reputation, I didn't feel that at all; rather a void of emotion of any kind. To date, he had raised $40 million or so through angel funding and venture capital Series A and B stages, so I knew the idea was early.

Later that day at a cocktail reception in the Grand Hotel Belvedere, I spent time with Accel's Jim Breyer to advance what felt like a miss with Mark. Accel had made the first sizable investment in Facebook following Peter Thiel's initial $500,000.

As it turned out, Facebook decided to wait another five years before going public in a deal valued close to $100 billion. I lost the opportunity to personally connect with a bunch of CEOs who were valued clients where I already had prepared talking points and a lot of relevance. Not to say I wouldn't do it again, it was risk taking that sent me home to our TMT team empty handed.

Understand risks, but know that you can't get anywhere without taking them.

CHAPTER 10

REINVENTING

ON APRIL 19, 1991, I was sitting with former heavyweight champion George Foreman in his locker room at Convention Hall in Atlantic City, New Jersey. He had just lost to the undefeated current heavyweight champion Evander Holyfield in a unanimous decision. The fight was billed as the Battle of the Ages.

The makeshift locker room had blue curtains separating it from a hallway. Big George was dejected. He was sitting motionless in a chair at the end of the locker room with a white shower towel over his head for an eternity. Unknown to me at the time, Evander had already concluded a post-fight interview and a press conference, and ESPN had reported that they heard George say "this was the end" as he left the ring. The media desperately wanted an interview to confirm his retirement.

George didn't say a word. He just sat there. Security kept the media out. Even Donald Trump, who had promoted the fight, with Marla Maples by his side, who poked through the blue curtain, was told, "Not now." Donald Trump hollered his supportive good wishes and left. Big George raised his arm in acknowledgment but didn't remove his towel that hid his dejection.

We sat in silence. It felt awkward and long. The former heavy-weight champion had raised the hopes of millions and millions around the world that if you had the will, there was a way. He didn't fight for himself. He fought for everyone who was told they were too old and, more broadly, for everyone who didn't believe in themselves. It was the highest grossing boxing match of all time because he was a disciple of hope. And he lost.

An aggressive cameraman with a bright light barged through the locker room's blue curtain. My business school buddy, Jonathan Jackson, who was sitting with me in silence, has a black belt in empathy. He was not about to let someone else define George by capturing his private post-fight misery on film. Jonathan had previously told me how the Ugandan dictator Idi Amin Dada would greet heads of state and dignitaries in a lodge that had a tiny entrance door and position his photographer at the door so that they could photograph them as Idi Amin helped them to their feet. Jonathan was very aware of the power of perspective.

Jonathan took matters into his own hands and began a boisterous monologue directed at the beaten boxer as the camera rolled:

> Big George! You're the champ. You're the people's champ.
>
> You just stood toe to toe with the heavyweight champion of the world.
>
> He's in his twenties, you're in your forties.
>
> He couldn't drop you; he was hanging on to you.
>
> You proved to everyone, we can all go toe to toe with the champions of the world.
>
> You proved it to everyone who is told they are too old.

> You proved it to everyone who is told they are too poor.
>
> You proved it to everyone who is told they are the wrong color.
>
> You proved it to everyone who is told they come from the wrong country, the wrong neighborhood.
>
> You proved it to everyone who doesn't believe in themselves.
>
> You proved it to all of us. We can all do it.
>
> You're the people's champion of the world!

On cue, after a seemingly endless period of mourning, George flipped the towel off his beaten bald head and stood tall and proud and marched toward the cameraman. In his words, he preached the gospel of hope proven by his performance in the ring.

In an instant, Big George, with help from Jonathan, redefined what had just happened in the Battle of the Ages and reinvented himself. Defeated to inspirational global hero.

At the next fight of his that I attended, he became the oldest heavyweight champion of all time when he defeated Michael Moorer at the MGM Grand Garden Arena on November 5, 1994.

Shortly thereafter, he endorsed the George Foreman Grill on the platform of hope and sold over a hundred million units earning him hundreds of millions of dollars, greatly exceeding what he made in his spectacular boxing career.

On a more pedestrian business dimension early in my business career, on a winter afternoon in 1995, the Operating Committee of our Wall Street firm gathered in the boardroom at 3 World Financial Center.

The then chief administrative officer (CAO) of our firm presented the status of our entry-level recruiting performance. The assessment presented only two factors to describe the entry-level class: GPA and SAT. And, since they were up on average versus the prior year for the entry-level class, the CAO declared victory.

I looked around the room. Out of all of us, only the executive with oversight of the recruiting process and presenting his version of recruiting performance (a Harvard alum himself) would have made it through the recruiting funnel process.

We were hiring the candidates rejected by our top competitors from the twenty schools where we recruited. Further, we were only describing our entry-level class by one dimension/competency: intellectual capability. There was nothing that addressed leadership, teamwork, determination, or diversity, which were all elements that a high-performing organization would have.

There had to be a better way.

I launched a side project away from the firm's recruiting function to see if there was a better way. We started by getting the résumés of every one of our 1,500 managing directors to see what they had in their background at the time they graduated from university. With the data, we ran correlations against markers to identify predictors of success. We determined that among the universe of variables, having been a student-athlete in college contributed most powerfully to likelihood of success (more so than outstanding verbal or math SAT scores, GPA, quality of university, work-study, or being elected class president or other offices). We targeted Academic All Americans, Rhodes scholars, Academic All-Ivy League, Academic All-Big Ten, and other conferences. Every recipient was readily identifiable.

We used a mass mail merge process to write each student-athlete a personally signed letter, congratulating them on their accomplishment and inviting them to explore a career in investment banking. Most student-athletes replied. Once we had their résumés, we cross-checked for the rest of our desired attributes. Most of the candidates who submitted résumés were eliminated from the process because they didn't have the complete set of qualifications we were looking for. However, we now had access to a universe of candidates who were outside the scope of our prior narrow process.

By reinventing the recruiting process, we were able to create a new methodology that

- expanded the addressable market by starting with a much larger universe of initial candidates (all graduates in the United States versus twenty schools);

- created a candidate screening process that began with a marker correlated to long-term success versus candidate interest level;

- reduced the cost of hiring candidates by over 50 percent;

- improved our recruiting competitiveness (our cross-offer win rate versus Goldman Sachs increased from 0 to 50 percent and versus Morgan Stanley from 25 to 70 percent);

- increased the quality of our hires; and

- built a new foundation of diversity at the firm.

Prior to this, we had never hired an Academic All-American student-athlete. We hired six in the first pilot. Drew Brees, NFL Super Bowl champion quarterback, was one of the recipients of my letter in this pilot program. It's pretty clear he made the right choice by ignoring me.

Over the next five years, we expanded the targeting to include other markers for success at our firm, such as academic accomplishment and leadership experiences. For example, we would have never found the valedictorian from Ohio State University who had a 4.0 GPA and 1,590 SAT scores and who was the math and physics student of the year. Through this process, we hired her without setting foot in Columbus, Ohio. There were hundreds of similar examples.

Several years later, this method of recruiting accounted for half of our entry-level recruits in the class of 1,000+ newly hired analysts. The candidates whom we targeted tracked ahead of their traditional on-campus recruited peers after two to three years despite their perceived university pedigree disadvantage.

By leveraging analytics and technology, we reengineered our entry-level recruiting processes that had been the standard for decades to create a much lower-cost, higher-quality engine.

No matter how small or big the project, consider reinventing it to expand the impact. The technology foundation upon which organizations sit evolves, and that creates continuous opportunities for reinvention. Opportunity is omnipresent.

As H. Jackson Brown Jr. said, "Seek opportunity, not security. A boat in harbor is safe, but in time its bottom will rot."

CHAPTER 11

PLANNING

ON NOVEMBER 14, 1993, my brother and I lined up for our first of a bunch of marathons together in Staten Island along with over 26,000 runners.

For the past two years, my brother had gloated about having run the New York City marathon and chided me for never having achieved the feat; perhaps my body was too fragile to sustain the distance. The constant provocation got the best of me. Sign us up, which he did. Now, having never run more than seven miles in my life, I asked him about the experience and need for training. People in my office planned for the event and trained every day for a year. He said,

> Scott, think about it. These are bankers who haven't worked out a day in their lives. Of course, they're training. And of course, they're whining. They never did three-a-day practices like we did for soccer or ran two 45-minute halves in the sand on the beach. They've never experienced pain, so they whine.

I bought it.

It was a brisk fifty degrees, so we wore sweatpants and sweatshirts; at the last minute, we told a friend to meet us at mile sixteen with a pair of shorts just in case. We hadn't checked the weather forecast. My training had my body in good five mile run shape and my oblivious spirits looking forward to tearing New York up.

Bang! Off we went. We started relatively close to the front behind the elite runners. We ran across the Verrazano-Narrows Bridge, which is actually a pretty healthy climb to the middle of the bridge; adrenaline was flowing. My brother told me to slow down; I complied but felt like a racehorse being held back. Then, down the bridge and through Brooklyn. At mile five, we checked and saw that we were running faster than a six-minute-thirty-second-per-mile pace. We had gone out way too fast; that was a sub three-hour marathon pace. At mile eight, I said, "We just ran the longest I've ever run." At mile nine, I was steaming hot and tired; 17.2 miles to go.

We threw our hats and sweatshirts to the side of the road, good riddance; unfortunately, we were still wearing sweatpants. I was dehydrated and looked for a water station; my brother had started hydrating much earlier. At the next station, I chugged a bottle yet was already looking for the next station.

The parties and bands along the sidewalks of the race route were turning from celebratory music to much-needed encouragement. The run through Brooklyn took forever. We noticed a man in a full head to toe green Gumby costume about to pass us. Heck no. There's no way that guy's passing us. We forced ourselves to pick up the pace.

Finally, we saw the 59th street bridge. Thank God, we were entering Manhattan.

My feet were hurting. A thin green carpet on the bridge did little to soften the pounding on the metal grating ground with each step.

Each step hurt, as my socks were wet from sweat and had created blisters that were beginning to sting.

The climb up to the middle of the bridge felt pronounced and squeezed much of what was left in my empty tank.

No dinner the night before, no breakfast, no sleep. My father had invited us to watch the #1 Florida State Seminoles play the #2 Notre Dame Fighting Irish in South Bend, Indiana, scheduled the day before the marathon. The game was marketed as the Game of the Century. That's a moment not be to missed, so we cheered the Irish to victory and headed to Chicago's O'Hare airport sans dinner immediately after to make the last flight to New York. We got to bed in New York around 1:30 a.m. and had to be up at 6 a.m.

As we approached Manhattan, we heard a thunderous welcome ahead. Massive crowds. We were running toe to toe with Gumby.

At every water station heading up First Avenue, we doused ourselves with water and chugged. My body was exhausted, hungry, and thirsty. At the sixteen-mile mark, we stopped at the rendezvous corner on First Avenue to meet the friend. Oh no, they grabbed the wrong shorts. These were my high school shorts that, for whatever reason, were still in my closet and last fit me about a decade ago. My legs were red and soaked from a run that was more than double the longest of my life at this point. I undressed on the ground in the middle of the crowd and jammed myself into the shorts. My thighs had chaffed and were bleeding. My feet were stinging. My nipples were raw. Every muscle was hurting. Spectators helped me to my feet.

We headed up First Avenue; the sun beat down on us. The temperature had increased by over twenty degrees since the start of the race. It was the hottest New York Marathon in memory, reaching 72.9 degrees in mid-November. We needed to get to a station for Vaseline for my thighs. I could barely stride. Thank goodness, a tub of Vaseline at a station. My hand grabbed as much from the tub as possible and lathered everything in my shorts to stop the stinging and chaffing. A burning sensation ensued. It can't be. Turning around to look at the label on the tub, it read: Bengay. My undercarriage was on fire.

The next five miles were rough. We headed into Queens and Harlem and then back into Manhattan. In Central Park, we encountered a hill. I told my brother, "Look at my thigh; you can see the quad muscle flickering. I have to stretch it." Kicking my right foot up behind me to grab it with my hand to stretch my quad muscle, my right hamstring cramped. The pain threw me to the ground. Immediately, my left hamstring and left calf went into a ball and cramped. What ensued next was an unending period of time writhing in pain on the ground, tossing and turning like a fish out of water. My bicep then cramped. I felt like Pheidippides after his last run from Marathon to Athens and had miles to go. At some point, the cramping stopped.

My brother and spectators again helped me to my feet. My brother graciously stuck with me and we walked, jogged, walked. Cramps threatened: stop. My body was spent. Collapsing on the ground and never getting up seemed like the only rational thing to do. Gumby was long gone, and I was pathetic. The last three miles were at a glacial pace. Everyone in New York City was passing us. Spectators strolling with baby carriages on the sidewalk were going faster than us.

Enduring pain is something that is required to get to many of life's finish lines. Much of this one was avoidable.

We crossed the finish line together ten minutes over the four-hour mark of dishonor. I collapsed on a stretcher in the first-aid area at the finish. After an extended period of laying there, a first responder told me "Either go to the hospital in an ambulance or get up and walk home." The humiliation of an ambulance was too much to bear for historical record. I limped out of the park and continued to limp for ten days.

Spontaneity can be good for some things. Marathon running certainly isn't one of them.

Life's a journey worth planning.

ETHICS

A MAJOR FIRM ON WALL STREET was struggling. They had a great business that our Wall Street firm didn't have. As a result, we had done the analysis on acquiring them, and it looked like a good strategic complement to our business, and the math worked.

The next step was for our CEO, to meet their CEO. I had my final briefing session with our CEO the morning before his dinner at the other CEO's apartment. I couldn't wait to hear what had happened when we met the following day. This was going to be a transformational acquisition.

Our CEO gave me a detailed account the morning after. To my naive surprise, their CEO cared about one thing: himself.

Our CEO: "So, what are your plans? What do you want to do?"

To which their CEO replied, "I don't care about the premium you pay (meaning the final purchase price above the then current stock price). My number is $100 million."

"Meaning?" probed our CEO.

"You can do it many ways. You can set me up with a multi-billion-dollar fund to manage and create a consulting agreement for the balance."

What did he mean by that? The math on carving out a $5 billion fund for him to manage as part of the transaction would be that he would make 2 percent in management fees on the $5 billion every year plus 20 percent of the annual profits that it generated (a standard in the industry called "2 and 20"). If he only invested conservatively and made a 5 percent return per year on the funds invested, he could use the 2 percent in fees, or $100 million per year, to rent the most lavish offices and pay for a fabulous team, and he'd personally pocket $50 million in profit sharing per year. A consulting arrangement of any sorts would be a cherry on top.

The deal was dead. Our CEO walked wanting no part of that.

Admittedly, I was shocked and had no idea that kind of stuff happened. It wasn't just the lack of ethics—rather the audacity of a leader (their CEO) to use the position so shamelessly in his self-interest. In a combination like this, the resulting entity would be stronger, more capable, and embark on a path of wealth and job creation. That being said, the near term is usually painful. A CEO is entrusted with the responsibility of their employees, including the financial well-being of them and, by extension, their families. In a combination like this, hundreds of employees would be fired in the near term. Hundreds of families would be affected. And the only thing this man could think of was his incremental $100 million personal gain. The behavior was beyond offensive.

Later, when another Wall Street firm announced the acquisition of that same company, I read in horror that the CEO was granted a package that included billions to establish a fund where he would be the managing partner and a $50+ million consulting contract over several years to advise the acquiring company. Incredibly, he succeeded in creating his personal economics despite his responsibility.

A couple years later, a friend called me telling me that senior employees at another Wall Street firm were just given the heads-up that a cover story in a major publication was going to read that their CEO was under pressure for his abysmal track record, including an unsupportive quote from one of the board members. Billions of dollars of market value had been wiped out during his short tenure.

I hung up the phone and worked on a financial model that showed the impact of our acquiring the firm. Before the end of the day, I walked into our CEO's office and said, "Another firm is in play; not the right strategic fit for us, but here's the proforma anyways."

A little over a month later, that firm too was acquired, and the CEO made off with a personal package that amounted to over $100 million.

Embarking on my career, I naively thought ethics beyond reproach at the top of corporate America was a given. Since then, I witnessed everything from admirable to deplorable.

Never compromise on ethics.

CHAPTER 13

ACCOUNTABILITY

I ENTERED A SMALL, DARK OFFICE overwhelmed with stacks of workbooks and pamphlets for my obligatory meeting with New Trier High School's college counselor. Sparing pleasantries in light of his packed schedule (my class had 1,350 students), he abruptly began the meeting. "What schools are you planning to apply to?"

My credentials at the time were a mixed bag on the backdrop of an unconventional upbringing with a great score in the math portion of the all-important SAT standardized tests but a miserable one on the verbal. Having grown up in Brazil and France, I had as much Portuguese and French language instruction as English through eighth grade, thus was woefully behind in English. My GPA was a 3.7 under New Trier's weighted system, anchored by a C+ in English and buoyed by As in two French advanced placement courses with varying flavors of grades in between.

With no idea how to respond to his question, I said, "Yale, my brother goes there. Georgetown, my sister goes there. Notre Dame, my dad went there. Northwestern?" In my family, there was no doubt that you went to the school that had the best academic reputation.

My immaturity and lethargy contributed to a pathetic level of project management on my part for such an important decision.

Universities are gateways to opportunity. The best universities provide the widest aperture of career choices.

The counselor responded, "Umm, those are all great schools. Maybe you should pick one of those as your stretch target and apply to some other schools where you are more qualified and then pick a safety school."

Fast-forward nineteen years to the spring of 2002, I flew to Chicago to go to the Chicago Club. It was an insanely busy time on Wall Street, but my dad's retirement from a thirty-year career at Booz Allen & Hamilton was an event I couldn't miss. The Chicago Club, founded in 1869, is a private social club located at Van Buren Street at Michigan Avenue.

Working the crowd of executives paying tribute to my father, a warm, familiar face stood out: Vicki Anderson. We hadn't seen eachother in about ten years. Vicki had been my father's executive admin for a couple decades. She threw me off at our encounter with a question. "Do you forgive me?"

"I beg your pardon? Why in the world would you ever have to ask me for forgiveness for anything?" Vicki had always managed a heavy balance of family matters and professional duties and done it all with alacrity.

"You know!"

"Uh, no, I don't. Truly."

"You know, when I transcribed (with a typewriter from my hand-written pages) your college application essays for you. I accidentally typed 'Northwestern' in every essay instead of the name of each individual school you applied to."

When my application response letters came in as a senior in high school, they were a steady stream of rejections: Yale, Georgetown, Notre Dame, and more.

The event, the people, the room, all disappeared for a moment. My mind drew up storylines of how my life might have been different had I been a more mature high schooler. In my professional life, I triple-check everything. On my college applications, I clearly hadn't checked the final version. Your reputation on Wall Street is highly correlated to never making a mistake; it is the cornerstone of your credibility.

I wished to have awoken earlier in life, including starting the college selection process earlier and approaching it with professionalism. This decision, more than any other, defines the set of opportunities that you are afforded when launching your career. I didn't select the college I wanted to attend. My laziness had selected my college for me.

Delegation is a requirement in life. A team gets more accomplished than the individual. Harnessing the different skills of each member of a team is critical in delivering outperformance across sports, business teams, community projects, and so on. One cannot and should not do everything. However, delegation must be done for the right reasons and with the right oversight considering the importance of the task. How you delegate something is up to you. Whatever the result, you own it because that was your decision.

Responsibility and accountability go together.

CHAPTER 14

PREPAREDNESS

IN 2006, I ATTENDED the Annual Meeting of the World Economic Forum in Davos, Switzerland. The attendees usually include something like 50 heads of statc, 100 ministers, 600 CEOs, and founders of companies, so the opportunity to speak directly with lots of decision-makers is like no other conference in the world.

The four-day affair is a plethora of choices. The official program affords the opportunity to listen to global experts and world leaders on a range of topics. Unofficially, there are countless invitations to breakfasts, lunches, dinners, and after-dinner events.

Among my invitations was a lunch hosted by Rijkman Groenink, chairman and CEO of ABN Amro. Jean Claude Trichet, the head of the European Central Bank, was the marquee guest attendee. I really looked forward to it. There were ten of us at a round table. Every other industry attendee was a CEO of an institution larger than mine. What happened next was a wake-up call.

The conversation was a central bank policy master class. I was so out of my league. I looked for opportunities to engage—whether a comment or a question. Each time, there was a gap in my knowledge that could expose my ignorance. These were things that I should have known as the representative of a major Wall Street firm. I was the co-chief administrative officer at the time. Each participant had about fifty years of relevant experience and were putting it to the test among formidable intellectual adversaries—save one. I was weaponless, naked. The two-hour lunch was endless. I felt weak and just wanted to get out of there.

Just because you're invited doesn't mean that you belong.

The lunch reminded me of the Northwestern University track-and-field championships.

One team had two of the fastest sprinters on our football team, Rudy Germany (wide receiver) and Jankieth Gatewood (safety) plus two skinny freaks of nature. All ran ten-second hundred-yard dashes. They had already qualified for the finals.

As the runners were loading their car to drive to the stadium for the finals, they couldn't find one of the skinny freaks of nature. They ran into 620 Lincoln Street in Evanston, Illinois, where a couple of them lived and yelled in the hallways to anyone that could hear, "Who's got wheels? We need a runner right now!"

Several had pointed them to me. They found me loafing in my room. They inquired about my speed. I ran a 4.7 second forty-yard dash but had never run the hundred. Suddenly, we were in the car headed to the first 4 × 100 meter race of my life. It was clear who was the slowest of the bunch. They decided to have me run the second leg.

When the gun went off, eight men were flying around the track at never-before-seen speeds. It was quite shocking. I was in lane 5. They were coming at me so fast it was absurd. Next to me in lane 4? Curtis Duncan. Curtis was a wide receiver on the Northwestern football team who went on to be selected by the Houston Oilers in the 1987 NFL Draft. Curtis played his entire seven-year career with the Houston Oilers during the run and shoot era with fellow receivers Ernest Givins, Haywood Jeffires, and Drew Hill and quarterback Warren Moon. His best year as a pro came during the 1992 season when he caught eighty-two receptions for 954 yards, earning him a selection to the Pro Bowl. We got the baton at the same time. So silly.

The next handful of seconds took an eternity. I was in that dream where I was supposed to run from danger, and, while my legs were moving, I wasn't going anywhere. Finally, I told myself, "Just put one foot in front of the other—just walk!"

By the end of my horrifying leg of the race, Curtis had separated himself from me by what felt like a mile. Of course, it was embarrassing. However, it was more profound than that. It was a lesson in self-awareness and preparedness.

One year later, I was invited to be one of five participants for the opening plenary session in Congress Hall for the 2007 Annual Meeting of the World Economic Forum, along with Fortune 50 CEOs including Muhtar Kent of Coca-Cola, a Curtis Duncan of sorts in the business world. Standing in front of two thousand WEF-Davos Annual Meeting attendees, many of whom were recognizable from all their global media exposure, I had already anticipated the vulnerabilities in every word I uttered. Heck, I had even rehearsed in front of a mirror naked since someone told me that it was good preparation for the pressure and sense of alienation that speeches create. Clearly, with that audience, any flaw would be known by someone, if not by many, in the room. Preparation can create breakthroughs.

Achievement stands on a foundation of preparedness.

CHAPTER 15

AWARENESS

I OPENED THE FREEZER LOOKING for a bite to eat as a freshman in high school, only to see a large bottle of the plainly branded Popov vodka. My father typically drank Stolichnaya, which is packaged in a more elegant looking bottle. I actually had no idea which was more expensive; rather I just saw an opportunity to make a joke. I ceremoniously pulled the bottle of Popov out and made a joke about it being the harbinger for our family's financial misfortune and demise.

Unknown to me, my widowed grandmother (my father's mom who had very little financial means) who was staying with us for the first time in my life had given that to my dad as her housewarming gift to him. Her reaction and the ensuing feeling of shame are something I feel to this day upon recollecting the moment. At seven o'clock in the evening sometime in 1980, my shame committed me to a lifetime of awareness, or so I thought.

Fast-forward four decades, effective six o'clock in the morning on March 26, 2020, Governor Jared Polis of Colorado issued an official statewide stay-at-home order for residents. Only essential workers and specific circumstances for other citizens were excluded from the order. The coronavirus pandemic grinded our country to a halt.

Zoom, a video conferencing app, became one of the fastest growing apps of the pandemic. Meeting participants grew by 2900 percent. It was how so many of us communicated and engaged. It filled business and social needs created by the inability to engage face-to-face. It also launched a universe of embarrassment as private moments at home made their way onto screens around the world.

The stock market was in free fall.

The University of Chicago and Northwestern University business schools created a spontaneous curriculum of sorts where individuals were asked to speak to their communities on various topics. They asked me to speak to their students, faculty, and alumni about the differences between the market meltdown of the global financial crisis and the one we were experiencing during the pandemic.

Fortunately, I had just installed fiber optic cable and Wi-Fi connectivity inside and outside my mountain home immediately before the stay-at-home order came into effect, so gladly accepted.

Following a week of singular focus, the meeting kicked off promptly at eleven o'clock on a sunny morning from a picnic table in my yard in Aspen, Colorado. A few books, stuffed animals and fruits served as items best able to prop up my laptop to deliver the right angle for on screen presence.

I had rehearsed dozens of times. The connectivity was tested dozens of times.

This was so much easier than live speeches as you can read your speech on the screen, and, so long as you have rehearsed, the participants have no idea that you are actually talking with prepared remarks right in front of you.

My remarks addressed the task I was given. However, it was much more important to me than that. To me, it was about delivering a message of hope, optimism, and understanding, knowing that anyone who joined the session was going through an impossibly difficult time in their life. I just wanted to deliver one single hour of relief and hope.

As I waited for the session to begin, I could see the growing number of people joining the session, 27, 56, 105, 238, 315, 447. A professor from the University of Chicago Business School began to introduce me.

Connection lost.

It can't be. Impossibly bad luck. Are you kidding me?

The chronology of the next fifteen minutes of panic is a blur. I tried desperately to get back into the Zoom meeting to no avail. Disconnecting and reconnecting the Wi-Fi, turning the laptop on and off, texting with the technician who just installed this absurdly expensive system.

Rage and anger overcame desperation and futility. I later learned that the professor stalled for a full fifteen minutes. He then capitulated and ended the meeting.

My meager contribution was a further gift of annoyance and disappointment to anyone who bothered to waste their time and join the session.

At the time, our house was being renovated. My wife Isabelle, our three young children, three dogs, and I were all living in a 1,500-square-foot apartment over a detached garage on our property. Every household has a head of IT. Isabelle was ours and had overseen the property's technology installation. I stormed the overpopulated center of chaos to provide her with real-time user feedback.

The stay-at-home order, work stoppage on our home renovation, home and online schooling of three young children, massive weight gain, cramped living space, and extraordinary cost of technology that failed all came together to create a cocktail of emotions that should have remained in the bottle.

There are times in life when certain people are conquered by demonic forces. Flinging the door open, my demonic kidnapper delivered the feedback commentary on the recently installed technology. The sixty-second monologue of profanity that ensued would get kicked off even the most accommodating among cable shows. I can't think of a curse word that I've ever heard that was omitted by the evil spirits who temporarily took hold of me.

My children were stunned. The dogs scurried to safety under chairs and a coffee table. Throughout the demonic monologue, my wife was sporting a goofy grin. A most unexpected reaction. I stopped.

Unknown to me, immediately prior to my storming of the over-populated encampment, our children's school psychologist was in the midst of hosting a Zoom video conference session with all second graders as part of her weekly pandemic wellness check. She had just finished the last sentence of her assignment to the children: "Now, I want you to draw your feelings on your piece of paper to show what it feels like to you to be in your home during this pandemic." On cue, began the demonic monologue to my family, my dogs, and the unmuted second-grade Zoom audience on Leo's laptop.

As the situationally oblivious pronouncement came to its abrupt end, silence reigned. I scanned the room trying to decode the basis for the silence and Isabelle's goofy grin. Family members and dogs alike remained motionless. It was ominously quiet.

Leo broke the ten seconds of silence and proclaimed to his second-grade classmates and the school child psychologist on the unmuted Zoom call, "That was my dad."

George Thorogood sang a song that the child psychologist likely internalized about me. In his first refrain, he sang:

On the day I was born.

The nurses all gathered 'round.

And they gazed in wide wonder

At the joy they had found

The head nurse spoke up

Said, 'Leave this one alone'

She could tell right away

That I was bad to the bone.

The school child psychologist never brought up the demonic monologue Zoom incident. Phew.

A decade earlier, my first meeting with Michael Jackson was meant to be at Neverland Ranch, his 2,700-acre residence in Santa Barbara County that abuts the Los Padres National Forest.

The flower-bordered mile-long driveway had Disneyesque music piped in the entire way to the house. As you approach the main house, there is a courtyard and guest house nearby. I stayed in the guest house.

Upon entering the main house, there was a wax butler figure that held a manifesto of sorts. Summarizing, it spoke to the purity of children and deceit of adults.

A greeter at the door told me unfortunate news: "Mr. Jackson has been unexpectedly detained and will not be able to join for the weekend. He insists you enjoy the weekend at his home and looks forward to getting together as soon as possible." I decided to stay.

His study had a photo collection that filled an entire room with red leather albums organized like a Dewey decimal system library.

Eating in the dining room, one was captured by an oil painting of Michael leading dozens of children running on a grassy knoll. The dining service was impeccable. Frankly, I can't recall what I ate, in part, because there was so much to take in. Once dinner concluded, one of the dining attendants asked:

"Would you like to see a movie?"

"Sure—what do you have?"

"Whatever you'd like. Perhaps there's a movie playing in the cinemas that you haven't seen?"

What? Current releases? I thought, "Sure, but I don't know what's playing."

She proceeded to bring me a list of movies currently playing in cinemas around the country. I picked one and was told to meet at the railroad station. I thanked the dining staff and walked to the train station to ride a full-sized steam locomotive engine train waiting to take me to the movie theater. There were three trains on the property; this was the largest rail, named Neverland Valley Railroad. "Toot toot" and off we went.

Arriving at the movie theater stop, the train attendant asked if I wanted to walk across the wobbly bridge or swing on the rope across the ravine. It was dark, so it was a wobbly bridge for me. I bid my farewells to the locomotive staff.

Upon entering the movie theater, there was a concession stand thirty feet long with every conceivable confection. For me, it was my usual movie going accompaniments: Milk Duds, large popcorn, and Diet Coke.

Entering the movie room, there was a selection of about 300 seats. There was only one other business acquaintance of his with me. We sat in the middle. Knowing how unexpected and unconventional everything seemed to be, I forced myself to look up, down, right, left, and then behind me. Who knew what I'd discover. While the towering ceiling was impressive, it was what was behind me that caught my attention. On each side of the projector was a glass-enclosed bedroom, complete with nightstands, picture frames, and so on. The bedrooms appeared to be rooms whereby Michael could go to sleep watching a movie in a floor-to-ceiling windowed room with a view into the movie room.

After the movie, we took the train back, and I went to bed in the guest house. Admittedly a bit thrown off, as the door had no lock, propped a chair against the knob.

The next day was equally eye-opening—swimming in the pool under the waterfall, playing video games in a guest house converted into a game house with a couple hundred arcade games, visiting the zoo, and meeting Michael's favorite orangutan, named Patrick.

We made our way to the amusement park. There was a Ferris wheel, carousel, Zipper, Octopus, Pirate Ship, Wave Swinger, Super Slide, roller coaster, and bumper cars. I rode most of them by myself.

I went to Neverland, forcing myself to be present. I left Neverland, more aware.

A month later, I met with Michael at his suite in the Helmsley Palace in New York City. He stayed at length in a magnificent, gilded suite. I brought the head media banker from our firm with me as the topic was going to be Michael's desire to create Neverland Pictures; that kind of transaction fell under the purview of the investment banking division. I was in executive management of the firm and made connections to our bankers but reserved working actively on deals for those situations where we were buying companies for ourselves.

Michael was no ordinary man on any dimension. He was the ground-breaker and music-performing standard setter of my generation. He was the king of pop. Yet, he did not conform to any of my expectations.

Mentally, he was a visionary. Yet he could not keep his eyes open for any business detail.

Professionally, he was driven. Yet, he rated himself as unaccomplished. Like many overachievers, he thought he had not yet created a legacy.

Fashion, he was straight out of the pages of a *Vogue* magazine you might pick up in a decade.

Physically, his skin appeared bleached, face subject to excessive plastic surgery, and every finger was bandaged. He had a most gaunt physique, almost skeletal.

Spiritually, he seemed to reside in a childlike utopia of fantasy.

At our meeting at the Helmsley, following pleasantries, I wanted to lay the foundation of capital alternatives before we dug deep on the feasibility of executing his vision. Within a minute or two, his eyelids began to close. Fearing I'd lose him, I took a hard pivot. "It reminds me of when I was a kid in São Paulo, Brazil."

His eyes opened and he leaned forward, "I love Brazil. I love Brazilians."

He launched into his vision. Paraphrasing him, he said, "Music is temporary. Pictures are permanent. Think about Grace Kelly, Fred Astaire—they will live on forever. I want to do the same. Music doesn't stand the test of time like movie pictures. That's why I want to create Neverland Pictures. And the first thing I want to do is buy Marvel comics and turn them into movies."

Awareness requires an open and available mind. Distractions, embedded standards of behavior, and expectations can limit your ability to capitalize on opportunities in life. Being present in the moment is difficult but correlates highly with productivity.

Our banker was never present and declined to give it any further consideration. Years later, Disney independently thought that was a pretty good idea and acquired the rights to Marvel for $4 billion. Disney proceeded to make over fifty Marvel movies.

If something merits time, it merits presence.

CHAPTER 16

LOVE

IN 1993, I was driving with Mo Siegel, the founder and CEO of Celestial Seasonings, in Boulder, Colorado. We were taking his company public, and I was an investment banker on the deal team.

Mo is a blond-haired, always smiling, free, fun, and loving spirit who cherishes the outdoors. He founded and ran the company that now serves more than 1.5 billion cups of tea per year. His venerable teas include Sleepytime, Raspberry Zinger, Mandarin Orange Spice, Bengal Spice, and so many more.

He liked me and wanted to share his wisdom with me even if it was before my time. He leaned toward me, squinted his eyes ever so slightly, and gave me the keys to his kingdom.

"You want a great marriage," he said. "To keep on succeeding in business, you need a great marriage. Every once in a while, not too often, but maybe every six to twelve months, get close to her and look into her eyes."

As he was confiding in me, he was displaying the facial expression and the thoughtful seriousness required to effectively succeed in the maneuver.

"Then say, 'I'm sorry.' She will know that you deserve to be sorry. You obviously won't know why you should be sorry. She'll want to know if you know why you should be sorry. So, the next part is critical. Move a little closer to her and look in an even more heartfelt and understanding way and say 'You know' then pause looking into her eyes and before she has the opportunity to engage verbally repeat 'You know' then hug her. It will work wonders for your marriage."

We all get lots of wonderful counsel, even if in jest. And, I am so appreciative of Mo's affection.

I think it's important to live life knowing why I fell in love, recalling all of the most amazing things about my wife. It's locked into my brain. It's a default mode, a worldview that helps put the relationship into context with every interaction. It's an explicit rationale that creates a foundation of perspective. I'll provide mine as an example. Here we go:

My wife is a diamond. There are many facets, each shining brilliantly at different times and from different vantage points.

First, I love that she loves me.

Global worldview. Isabelle has a macro lens in life. With education and experiences comes context. Every day, I am a beneficiary of the richness of Isabelle's worldview.

Intelligence. Isabelle has wonderful processing capability. She is constantly learning because she has an insatiable appetite and capacity to learn.

Ingenuity. My favorite paintings are the ones Isabelle created. My favorite house is the one Isabelle designed. Isabelle's ingenuity is a gift, and my life is enriched by it.

Grace and elegance. Isabelle has a rare refinement. Her femininity begs chivalry. I assume that attending a boarding school where she had to eat with her arms behind a broomstick on her back contributed to her grace and elegance.

Determination. Isabelle has established herself as a new economy trailblazer. Her vision, courage, and ability to break new ground are striking. Among her many milestones, Isabelle is the youngest ever female chairman of a New York Stock Exchange traded company.

Beauty. They say beauty is in the eye of the beholder. That being said, I can't think of a party, cocktail, dinner, club, or event where Isabelle wasn't the belle of the ball. As one Frenchman told his friend as she walked by his table, "Quelle merveille de beauté."

Isabelle is my diamond. She is my partner for life.

I've found it useful to document my choice in a partner and to use it as a foundation for interactions in and outside of marriage.

Make love last.

CHAPTER 17

BALANCE

ONE DAY, MY POPS (my father) was in Manhattan. He wanted to see me. I offered him a lunch slot, which was unheard of for me because I always ate at my desk. On the short cab ride to the India House in Lower Manhattan, I told him over the phone what to order for my main dish. My Pops had his appetizer without me. I arrived, wolfed down the entree in record time, and left in under ten minutes. Unable to immediately find a cab, I jogged back to the office.

My boss once told me, "Mediocrity is like the lollipop of life, one lick and you suck forever." I was committed to never taking a lick of that lollipop.

Wall Street meant suspending or jettisoning virtually everything in life. "No" was my response to everything and everyone other than work for eighteen years, beginning with my summer associate internship.

My summer associate internship in the investment banking division at Merrill Lynch typified the experience. In my interview prior to joining, I communicated my willingness to work as many more weeks as they'd like beyond the standard ten weeks, but that there was one week in the middle of the summer that I needed to take off for a long-standing family commitment. They said it wasn't a problem. Fifteen years earlier in 1975, we had celebrated my tenth birthday at the same restaurant in Venice, Italy, that my parents had celebrated their engagement fifteen years before then in 1960. My father told our family then that no matter where each of us was in life, we would all get back together at this same restaurant fifteen years later in 1990. We all committed.

Good fortune had it that the 1990 World Cup was being hosted by Italy that summer. That's only happened twice ever. We had tickets to a quarterfinal, semifinal, and the final game.

That summer, I was working eighteen hours a day, seven days a week, at Merrill Lynch in New York. All my time was dedicated to the restructuring of Southland Corporation, owner of 7-Eleven stores, which had 13,000 locations worldwide, including 7,000 in the United States. The company had taken on too much debt and couldn't meet its interest payment obligations.

My role was running the financial model. My biggest challenge was the size and complexity of the model. After every negotiating session with the company or the creditor committee with bankers led by Ken Moelis and Nate Thorne, who regularly came up with lots of potential solutions, I'd have to build all the options and contingencies into the financial model. The model had over 50,000 cells.

At one point, we had so many decision tree forks in one of the cells (the one relating to how much cash would be attributable to a senior tranche of indebtedness) that the cell in my spreadsheet wouldn't accept any more characters. It was a Lotus 1-2-3 spreadsheet program. The maximum number of characters in any given cell was 255. I couldn't fit all the required decisions (if-then statements) into the cell and didn't want to create a new referenced page elsewhere as that would create more complexity. Cell EZ113 was the bane of my existence.

My three to four hours allocated per day to sleep were consumed with dreams about the spreadsheet and cell EZ113.

My best day? Waking up in the middle of the night having solved the problem in cell EZ113 during a dream.

My worst day? After having solved the EZ113 problem, being told I couldn't go on the family trip that was fifteen years in the making—not even for one day.

Eighteen years later, our wedding reception was in southern France during the last week of August 2008. We had rented a place for ten days and had planned a full week of activities.

The week of my departure, my boss walked into my office and said, "I've got good news and bad news for you. Which one do you want first?"

It was August 2008. Over the past year, our firm had been getting pounded daily in the press and suffered a stock price per share decline from the $60s to the mid-teens. At that point, handling bad news was as habitual as getting my morning cup of coffee. "Bad news. Bring it."

"This thing in France … you can't go."

I looked at him incredulously. "You mean my wedding reception? For which, Isabelle and a dozen of her friends are already there and one hundred people are coming? *That* thing?"

"Yeah, that thing."

"What's the good news?" I asked.

"I need you." He left my office.

I skipped the week in France and, instead, flew on a red-eye Friday night, landed the day of our wedding reception, and returned to New York on Sunday morning immediately following the reception.

This was my first missed weekend at work in about six months. The last time I missed a weekend at work was when I took Isabelle to Turks & Caicos and was on the phone the entire weekend as Bear Stearns took its last breath as an independent company.

Naturally, I was the last passenger to board the plane Friday evening, having cut it dangerously close to departure time. To make matters worse, the red-eye was painful as I was traveling with a freshly broken hip.

Before I knew it, my precious hours away from the office had expired, and I was on a plane headed back to New York wondering what had just happened. There was no honeymoon.

That framework kept me at work on Wall Street for an average of over ninety hours per week over an eighteen-year period.

While I was making eight figures, the firm collapse combined with the pay structure (where virtually all my compensation was in stock with five-year sales restrictions) wiped me out. Nearly two decades of total commitment and I was about to be broke. I had to start over.

It took me a long time to figure it out, but balance matters.

My Pops once said to me, "Have a home where you love it so much you don't want to leave. And have a job for which you feel the same."

Take that thought, but apply it to much more than just work and family. Construct a portfolio approach to life. Define each of the aspects of your life for which you want to dedicate time—for example, family, professional, spiritual, fitness, friends, not-for-profit endeavors, culture, and travel. Then for each allocation of time, plan for that slice of your life, one that you can't wait to get to and don't want to leave once you are there. Each slice should be a highlight of life. It took me a long time to figure that one out, but I'm much happier now that I got it.

Balance can lead to a life with constant fireworks of happiness and fulfillment.

C H A P T E R   1 8

TRANSMISSION

TAKING MY SEAT in an auditorium on W 63rd Street on the south side of Chicago, two blocks west of South Ashland Avenue, I could see the jousting of folks trying to squeeze into the frames of cameras focused on my mom and Mayor Daley of Chicago. It was blue ribbon cutting time and the official opening of the newly built state-of-the-art Mitzi Freidheim Englewood Child & Family Center.

Englewood has a poverty rate of 45 percent. Unemployment is ten times the national average. Three-quarters of residents live with food insecurity risk. Infant mortality is over triple the national average. There is a one-in-ten chance for residents of becoming a victim of a violent crime. It's known as Chicago's murder capital, with daily shootings and an average of seventy homicides per year. The movie *Chiraq* was filmed in Englewood.

The center is a 32,000-square-foot beacon of hope in Englewood's midst that serves 261 children and families each year with programs including Head Start, child care, computer literacy, General Educational Development (GED) parental education, and more. Their mantra is help, hope, and opportunity.

My mom lives by an admirable personal code; within it, one behavior she shared with me long ago: "Do one unexpectedly kind thing for someone every day." I've seen her in action on a daily basis; this just happened to be a big one.

When one of the dignitaries said, "This light of hope is needed now more than ever, in Chicago, in Illinois and in our nation. Mitzi exemplifies what it means to be a 'lamplighter' for children," it hit me. She has been that for me, and I've got a lot of catching up to do.

Passing on your values to the next generation is at the core of the civilized circle of life. Lots of things are predetermined biologically, but the words and actions of adults will most impact the next generation. My childhood happened to be blessed with adoring parents, and my heart aches for those whose childhood has been torturous.

We all have our own set of values and traditions; however, we all share one extraordinarily precious transmission vehicle, bedtime.

Children's books aren't just about the story and drawings. They are about the experiences they create when cuddling with your children as you read to them as they go to sleep and reinforcing the foundation you desire to establish for them. You have the enjoyment of curating from others' masterpieces.

Many have lessons worthy of a lifetime of reflection. Pick what you want. Three masterpieces stand out to me.

The Little Prince by Antoine de Saint-Exupery:[1]

> "People where you live," the little prince said, "grow five thousand roses in one garden... yet they don't find what they're looking for ... And yet what they're looking for could be found in a single rose ..."

---

1   Antoine De Saint-Exupery, *The Little Prince* (New York: Reynal & Hitchcock, 1943).

A rock pile ceases to be a rock pile the moment a single man contemplates it, bearing within him the image of a cathedral.

... eyes are blind. You have to look with the heart. The most beautiful things in the world cannot be seen or touched, they are felt with the heart.

... I must endure the presence of a few caterpillars if I wish to become acquainted with the butterflies.

Oh, the Places You'll Go! by Dr. Seuss:[2]

You have brains in your head. You have feet in your shoes. You can steer yourself in any direction you choose. You're on your own. And you know what you know. And YOU are the one who'll decide where to go ...

You're off to Great Places!

Today is your day!

Your mountain is waiting,

So ... get on your way!

So be sure when you step, Step with care and great tact. And remember that life's A Great Balancing Act. And will you succeed? Yes! You will, indeed! (98 and ¾ % guaranteed) Kid, you'll move mountains.

---

2   Theodor Seuss Geisel, *Oh, The Places You'll Go!* (New York: Random House Books, 1990).

The Giving Tree by Shel Silverstein:[3]

And after a long time, the boy came back again.

"I am sorry, Boy," said the tree, "but I have nothing left to give you—

My apples are gone."

"My teeth are too weak for apples," said the boy.

"My branches are gone," said the tree.

"You cannot swing on them,"

"I am too old to swing on branches," said the boy.

"My trunk is gone," said the tree.

"You cannot climb—"

"I am too tired to climb," said the boy.

"I am sorry," sighed the tree.

"I wish that I could give you something ... but I have nothing left. I am an old stump. I am sorry ..."

"I don't need very much now," said the boy, "just a quiet place to sit and rest. I am very tired."

"Well," said the tree, straightening herself up as much as she could,

---

3   Shel Silverstein, *The Giving Tree* (San Francisco: Harper & Row, 1964).

"Well, an old stump is good for sitting and resting. Come, Boy, sit down. Sit down and rest."

And the boy did.

And the tree was happy.

Transmission of values is important.
Bedtime is magical.

CHAPTER 19

HAPPINESS

IN 2011, I sat down for dinner at the Hotel Cresta Sun in Davos, Switzerland, with the president of Nigeria. At the dinner, President Goodluck Jonathan talked about a recent study that ranked Nigerians as the happiest people on the Earth—this, in spite of the country being ranked 104th on the 2011 Legatum Prosperity Index and with a gross national income per capita of around $2,000 per year.

President Jonathan explained that most Nigerians live in very modest homes in crowded cities and towns. When they get up in the morning and go out their front door, all they can see are other Nigerians coming out of homes that are much like theirs. There is little disparity in terms of standard of living, so they don't long to be in someone else's shoes.

Frankly, I found the logic delusional and removed from tragic realities of the plight of so many living in poverty. More broadly, it also concerned me how some elites justify tolerance and acceptance of things that should be addressed. However, it brought my attention to something I rarely considered: happiness.

The fourteenth Dalai Lama said that human happiness and human satisfaction must ultimately come from within oneself. It is wrong to expect satisfaction to come from money or from a computer. He has pointed to a Tibetan saying, "[A]t the door of the miserable rich man sleeps the contented beggar." The point of this saying is that happiness comes from setting limits to one's desires and living deliberately within those limits.

Wall Street is a fabulous training ground for learning business and surrounds you with many of the brightest people. Yet, it has a shortcoming as it relates to happiness. Wall Street establishes that your value is defined by your compensation, and there is a great disparity in compensation. When I worked on Wall Street, in 2007, our firm had employees making as little as $25,000 and as much as $50 million for that year. The 1000th highest paid employee was paid $1,500,000. We had lots making lots and lots making little. Wall Street is an all-consuming place for all yet not a particularly happy place for most.

I have met thousands of people. On almost all occasions I have asked the following:

- How's it going?
- What are you up to? or
- How can I help you?

Not once in my lifetime has anyone ever said, "Fine, thank you, I'm pursuing happiness." Or, "Thanks for asking, I'm pursuing happiness and maybe you could help." In fact, if anyone did, you might think they are a kook. It's not a socially accepted goal.

Happiness is important. So much so that it is in the second sentence of the Declaration of Independence of the United States: "We hold these truths to be self-evident, that all men are created equal, that they are endowed by their Creator with certain unalienable Rights, that among these are Life, Liberty and the pursuit of Happiness."

The language says you have the right to pursue it, but researchers have noted that the founding fathers might have meant not just the pursuit but also the attainment. In the Virginia Convention's Declaration of Rights, just a few weeks before July 4, it talks about the "pursuing and obtaining" of happiness. Whatever it might have been, the founding fathers knew happiness mattered.

Pharrell Williams' song "Happy" has as its refrain this counsel:

Clap along if you feel like a room without a roof

Clap along if you feel like happiness is the truth

Clap along if you know what happiness is to you

Clap along if you feel like that's what you wanna do

While I don't know many people who haven't heard the song, I have never met anyone who said they live by it or anything close to it.

Meaning and purpose in life will contribute powerfully to happiness. In our society being ravaged by mental illness and suicides, it is more important than ever.

Life is filled with happiness. Pursue it unapologetically.

CHAPTER 20

RESPONSIBILITY

SITTING IN MY OFFICE on the thirty-first floor at 745 Seventh Avenue in New York City in the early evening, I reflected on where our firm stood.

On Tuesday, March 18, 2008, our firm had announced earnings. Although profits more than halved, the drop was less severe than Wall Street analysts had feared. In the quarter, we earned $489 million, down 57 percent on the previous year and equating to $0.81 per share. Analysts had forecast earnings per share at $0.72 per share.

Nevertheless, one could tell that the market had quickly shifted from focusing on our pursuit of Goldman as the leader on Wall Street to focusing on our ability to survive. All seven of the earnings call questions posed by the equity research analyst community revealed the concern. Here were the first two:

Q1: Meredith Whitney at Oppenheimer said that she really appreciated our disclosure and then asked whether a permanent buyer remained for securities not covered by the Fed facility. She also asked how our regulatory capital was faring.

Q2: Prashant Bhatia at Citigroup asked how Lehman planned to use the Fed facility—to reduce the debt level of the firm or to help clients do transactions. Then Prashant asked how we were doing on our capital plan.

The Motley Fool then published the first piece I can recall making the Bear Stearns (an already failed investment bank) analogy to our situation.

> Although Lehman has largely been able to sidestep major losses amid the subprime mess, like Bear Stearns, it does a disproportionately large amount of business in the fixed-income and mortgage-backed-securities market. For investors and clients facing Bear Stearns shares that now trade around 90% below their Friday closing, a similar 'run on the bank' on Lehman's assets isn't far-fetched.
>
> The same thing that drove Bear Stearns into the gutter is now Lehman's worst enemy: fear.[4]

As I looked out across the city, I focused on the single-most important thing we needed: delivering confidence. We had launched an equity raise to deliver on that. Our team led by Bart McDade, the chief operating officer, assembled a group of investors prepared to put equity capital in the firm. On a parallel track, we had discussions with Berkshire Hathaway, a banking client, for which we had a relationship with Warren Buffett's top lieutenant David Sokol. I wasn't directly involved in either of the work streams but had to weigh in.

Earlier that day, I told our CEO that my view was the power of having Buffett behind us superseded the benefits of better economics proposed by Bart from the more distributed institutional equity raise. He believed in the benefit but told me that every other executive committee member was telling him to go with the other investors.

---

4   Morgan Housel, "Is Lehman Brothers Next to Go?" April 5, 2017, https://www.fool.com/investing/dividends-income/2008/03/17/is-lehman-brothers-next-to-go.aspx.

Bart, supported by all executives reporting to him, convinced our CEO to take his recommendation.

Notwithstanding, I had an idea that would be my last desperate attempt prior to the public announcement. Perhaps by giving him a draft announcement of a Buffett investment, it would shed better light on how compelling it could be.

I picked up my phone and dialed Tim Lyons, our head of strategy, and I asked him to create a "Dear Colleague" letter to announce Buffett's investment in Lehman and outlined the messaging and flow of the announcement. I had never asked Tim to draft a communication piece, but this was so sensitive, so important, so urgent, and he was so sharp. He said he'd jump on it.

An hour later, Tim emailed me the memo I was looking for on March 27 around ten o'clock at night.

RICHARD S. FULD

CHAIRMAN AND CHIEF EXECUTIVE OFFICER

March 28, 2008

Dear Colleague,

Over the past decade, we have built a premier global investment bank that is well positioned to deliver industry-leading growth and profitability across all parts of the market cycle. In building this franchise, we have made significant investments in each of our divisions and regions to build our capabilities so that we can deliver superior products to our clients and capture share in the most attractive markets around the world.

The current market environment has obviously created significant challenges for all players in our industry. Uncertainty about the value of financial assets, combined with incomplete information and often inaccurate market rumors, has reduced the confidence of both debt and equity investors. So, it is an enormous tribute to the strength and growth of our franchise that Warren Buffett, the world's most respected investor, has decided to invest $3.5 billion in our Firm through Berkshire Hathaway. This investment will be made in the form of a perpetual non-cumulative preferred security with a coupon of 7.5% and a conversion price that is a 40% premium to our current stock price. The security is convertible into a 16% stake at the conversion price of $54 per share and is not callable for five years.

This strategic stake will provide us with additional capital to take advantage of the many attractive opportunities available to us in the marketplace, and at the same time, will increase the confidence of market participants in the strength of our Firm.

Our entire executive committee had also committed to receiving its entire 2008 incentive compensation in this same form of equity.

Over the years, Warren Buffett has distinguished himself as the world's most insightful and successful investor. Through Berkshire Hathaway, he has delivered long-term shareholder value, by investing in strong, high-performing, growth companies such as Coca Cola, American Express, Wells Fargo, General Re and GEICO.

I am thrilled to welcome Warren Buffett and Berkshire Hathaway as partners with all of us as shareholders in the

Firm and look forward to working together to capture the extraordinary opportunities that lie ahead of us.

Sincerely,

I showed the memo to our CEO. He liked it, but it seemed to me that he felt his hands were tied by Bart.

On Monday, March 31, we announced that we had raised $3 billion from a group of investors in an effort to quash the perception that there was inadequate capital. The shares rose by $5.32 to $42.96. The rise was ever so temporary.

I believe that had we secured an investment from Warren Buffett, the most successful investor in world history, Washington might have viewed Lehman Brothers differently. Perhaps the firm's demise could have been avoided. Goldman Sachs did it a few weeks later and lived to fight another day. As always, Warren Buffett made a fortune.

I don't know a lot. What I do know is that I had not earned the right to be the decision-maker on this and lots of other decisions throughout my career whether my views were good or bad.

Once the decision-maker, I only have myself to blame.

As Jack Nicholson said as Frank Costello in Martin Scorsese's *The Departed*, "Heavy lies the crown—sort of thing."

CHAPTER 21

QUO VADIS

I WAS AT A LUNCH of the Economic Club of New York at the Hilton in New York on October 15, 2008. It was the first meeting that our club hosted that I had been to in a long time. This one, however, was one of particular interest to me. The chairman of the Federal Reserve of the United States was speaking about the global financial crisis that dealt a financial blow to so many. Of course, I was most interested in his take, if he was going to say anything at all on it, on why the Fed decided not to support Lehman.

My last twelve months had been workdays averaging eighteen hours, seven days a week, with unrelenting, mounting, and suffocating pressure. The stress was extraordinary. The vice grip of doom had been tightening daily, and plastered all over newspapers around the world. My body had tightened to the point of ripping a tendon off my hip leaving me with a fractured hip. My net worth had vanished, my house was for sale, and my status was unemployed. Every ounce of my physical and mental capabilities had been left on the field trying to save the firm. So naturally, it was a speech of particular interest to try to make sense of it all.

The chairman of the Federal Reserve Bank did address it and said,

A public sector solution for Lehman proved infeasible as the firm could not post sufficient collateral to provide reasonable assurance that a loan from the Federal Reserve would be repaid and the Treasury did not have the authority to absorb billions of dollars of expected losses to facilitate Lehman's acquisition by another firm.

I immediately appreciated that "reasonable assurance" was subjective and provided decision-making latitude.

But I couldn't stop thinking; the firm's equity stood at $28 billion and had expanded its liquidity pool two days prior to the final weekend. It sure seemed to me that there was adequate collateral to secure a loan from the Fed.

But even if there wasn't, it's not as if Lehman sprang its desire for support from the Fed at the last second, leaving too little time to make a thoughtful decision. Quite the opposite.

In June 2008, months before the fateful weekend, several of us were huddled in our CEO's office on a call where he asked the Fed to allow us to become a bank-holding company. Among the dozens of work streams we had underway to get the firm out of harm's way, this call was the one we felt would single-handedly accomplish it. It was Rodge Cohen, senior chair of the law firm Sullivan & Cromwell, who gave us the idea when some of us met with him in our global headquarters boardroom at 745 Seventh Avenue a few days before the call.

The Fed could have allowed Lehman to become a bank-holding company at that point in time or any point in those months leading up to the final weekend. The Fed had employees in our offices full-time for months with access to everything, so they understood our deteriorating position real time for months. I recalled welcoming them to our firm and insisted that if they ever asked for anything whatsoever and did not get it immediately to call me. They never did.

The Fed said that becoming a bank-holding company would send the wrong message to the markets. As it turned out, months later, the Fed turned Goldman Sachs and Morgan Stanley into bank-holding companies sending the right message. That decision that saved Goldman, Morgan Stanley, and others was instrumental in preventing the collapse of the entire financial system.

I left lunch feeling empty.

After the collapse, some Lehman executives joined a claim against the estate to recover the equity that had been given to us, insisting that it was compensation that should be repaid to them as a trade payable, a senior claim on the estate. Along with some other executive colleagues, I did not join the claim despite their view that it was a free option to perhaps recover millions. One filed a claim for over $230 million. I thought it was wrong.

Similarly, a number of Lehman executives secured for themselves multi-million-dollar compensation guarantees in the sale of certain Lehman assets to Barclays. These same executives stood to make nothing if we survived. To make millions when the firm failed was also wrong in my view. When our CEO, who was not part of that group, asked me if I was interested in joining the group, I said, "No."

For Wall Street executives, myself included, to lose their jobs and virtually their entire net worth was right.

For Main Street to suffer so profoundly was not. The latter felt preventable.

It may seem as if I am condemning individuals at the Fed for the way they handled the global financial crisis. Definitely not. To me, they got close to everything they were empowered to get right. They saved a lot more than just the financial system. They were dealt a horrible hand as they focused on containing a financial firestorm.

I believe the barrier for them was that in the period leading up to Lehman's collapse, the Washington consensus (understanding much less than the Fed about the financial system and driven, in part, by political motivations) was that supporting a troubled financial institution would encourage more risky behavior and increase the need for further bailouts. They had already saved several other financial institutions. The political pressure to let the next bank fail was enormous.

The Fed reinforced the point themselves on the final Friday before Lehman went down, echoing what the US Treasury had been saying: "There is no political will in Washington for a bailout." Voila.

It seems to me, the world suffered, again in part, because of suffocating political pressure.

As we prepare for the next time—and there will be a next time even if it doesn't look exactly like 2008—Washington needs to remember this lesson and be prepared.

Quo Vadis is Latin for "Where are you going?"

A colleague of mine on Wall Street once said, regarding an assignment for a client (having nothing to do with Mexico), "If you want to go to Mexico, you at least have to be pointing in the right direction. And it's a long way to walk, so you may want to think about how you're going to get there too."

In the Bible, Saint Peter asks the risen Jesus that very question. His answer helps Saint Peter continue with his ministry and destiny. We certainly now have time to think that through and prepare accordingly to ensure we go where we want to go when it happens.

What do I think we should do?

We should consider convening a proper Basel IV (meeting of the Basel Committee on Banking Supervision to establish updated global standards for banks to follow) to ensure we established the right levels of controls on financial institutions. The current standards were put in place in a hurry following the crisis. Were they too loose or too constraining? Enough time has passed to assess.

We should consider depoliticizing Section 13(3) of the Federal Reserve Act and the Dodd-Frank Act so that the Fed, with its extraordinary talent, can protect us from another crisis. Post crisis, additional requirements were put in place that make it more difficult for the Fed to avert a crisis by supporting a failing entity.

And to avoid both the political pressure that can come with government support for a failing institution and American taxpayers from having to pay for the consequences, we should consider an industry-financed fund backed by the Fed that marries an institution's systemic risk level with their required level of contribution. That way, the next bailout will have been funded in advance by the banks, not the people.

I lost my job and virtually my entire life's savings. I was within spitting distance of being bankrupt after seventeen years of employment. And that was right.

U.S. taxpayers over the years have funded roughly 1,000 companies with about $700 billion. My view is that any company in any industry that requires to be bailed out by the Fed should automatically require every board member and the CEO and, perhaps, all of the direct reports of the CEO to be fired.

Lehman didn't deserve a bailout, nor did Morgan Stanley or Goldman Sachs. No company ever deserves a bailout.

However, Americans and, in this case, citizens of the world deserved Lehman to be bailed out like the other firms to avoid the depths of the global financial crisis that ensued and impacted so many so profoundly. Estimates of the cost of the global financial crisis hover around $10 trillion.

Starting with the destination will help in getting there.

C H A P T E R 2 2

STRATEGY

I WAS THE NEWLY APPOINTED president of Kenmore, Craftsman & Diehard staring at the business's five-year historical performance deterioration in market share and profitability.

Kenmore was a brand with no manufacturing; its primary manufacturers were LG, Samsung, Whirlpool, GE, Bosch, and Electrolux. I decided to meet with the CEOs or presidents at each of the manufacturing companies as part of my first thirty days' assessment. In my first meeting with the president of Samsung, I asked, "How many product developers do you have?" He said, "Five thousand." "Yikes," I thought.

We needed a new strategy fast because forty product developers in Hoffman Estates, Illinois, weren't going to cut it against the armies at each of the manufacturers. The storyline was the same across the business functions. We had two product designers. The CEO of Whirlpool told me they had 500.

We thought about the leverage we had and devised a new strategy. The entire team got involved. We would have speed brainstorming lunches in the cafeteria. I created a universe of generic strategies on an illustrative strategy wheel, and each team member would have sixty seconds to come up with their ideas. We'd go around and around the table for each strategy type. Everyone got involved. Everyone was vested in the creation of what we were to become.

When the query about what percentage of each manufacturer's capacity utilization was attributable to Kenmore, the answer that came back was great news. Typically, the manufacturer's plants were running at 85 percent capacity. Kenmore products generally accounted for about 25 percent.

Soon thereafter, I met with the head of the major appliances business of each of the manufacturers to explain that we wanted a better relationship than we previously had and asked for them to provide us with their three-year forward innovation road map. There was immediate pushback because revealing their future product was the most sensitive competitive information. However, we were only going to select manufacturers to produce Kenmore products from those that provided the innovation road maps. We could afford to lose some of them if push came to shove.

Our leverageable advantages were really twofold:

1. the high marginal utility that we delivered to them by adding capacity utilization to their manufacturing plants, and

2. we had a 30 percent market share in major appliance retailing in the United States at the time; thus, they needed us to sell their product.

It was hard to refuse our request because any business head who caused their plants to go from 85 percent utilization to 60 percent overnight would be in a difficult spot with their boss. Everyone complied.

As a result, we were able to handpick the best products from the manufacturers with full visibility of what innovation was coming in the years ahead from the industry. This led to the most formidable product line in the industry as well as in the history of Kenmore.

The strategy delivered transformational operations, market share, and financial results. We accelerated the innovation pipeline by 300 percent and improved quality across the brand extending our lead in Consumer Reports (double the number of #1 ratings versus our closest competitor). Kenmore improved from #3 market share (behind GE and Whirlpool) to #1 in the US.

The team was celebrated. Pride and morale surged. The doors to a new bright future of exciting options opened.

Think through where leverage exists. From there, much of the right strategy will fall into place.

C H A P T E R 2 3

FRIENDSHIPS

IT WAS NOVEMBER 5, 2022; our one win and seven losses Northwestern Wildcats were about to take the field against the undefeated, nationally celebrated Ohio State Buckeyes. The last time I had been to Evanston, Illinois, for a game against Ohio State was in 2004 with Isabelle when Northwestern won 33–27. We were underdogs then, so naturally I was not capitulating, notwithstanding our 38-point underdog status, according to Las Vegas bookkeepers.

Darnell Autry, former Heisman finalist from Northwestern who took us to the Rose Bowl, and I took a photo together with the Ohio State superfan outside the stadium and made our way to a pregame breakfast event. We socialized with the incoming and former university presidents, board members, alums, and staff and enjoyed the school spirit of the Northwestern University marching band and cheerleaders' performance. My son was loving hanging with Darnell and really appreciated hugging Willie the Wildcat again.

After the festivities, we made our way to the president's box. After a hard-fought first half, the game was knotted at 7–7. The halftime result was a remarkable feat. I thought, "Did it have to be that way?" So, I engaged Darnell on a universe of ideas that could creatively level the playing field. We iterated until we came up with what if the university allocates $1 billion of the university's $15 billion endowment to create 2,500 postgraduate guaranteed need–based income annuities for the most extraordinary academic and athletic high school graduates in the country.

That would attract the most talented academics and athletes to Northwestern because if they did not succeed post-graduation, notwithstanding their overwhelming attractive prospects at the time of joining the university, for whatever reason, they'd have guaranteed income.

Imagine the talent that would be attracted with the downside-protected value proposition. It seems no university in the country has ever done this; I hadn't thought it through completely but liked it on the surface. And as it relates to my passion for Northwestern football, this would improve our chances of making it back to the Rose Bowl by attracting the best student-athletes.

We brought the idea during the game to a board member of the university. I only hope he doesn't ignore the framework of the idea.

Long-term friendships are wonderful and should be protected and cherished. However, as my life progressed, I decided to relieve the pressure of having best friends who were required to play a role in many aspects of life. Instead, I created friendships across a range of elements that interested me. We get together to share the joy of one shared dimension of life.

Every one of our eight billion inhabitants on planet Earth has something special to offer. Be open to the idea that everyone may add to your life even if they only relate to you on one dimension of who you are or who you aspire to become.

Consider also defining nonnegotiables. What is it about a person who would make you decide you couldn't be friends with them? Draw a line. Even though it may be awkward on occasion, sever relationships that impede your mission to lead an honorable life.

"Walking with a friend in the dark is better than walking alone in the light."

—HELLEN KELLER

PRIORITIZE

I WAS ON A ONE-WAY FLIGHT from Chicago to London reading through research reports on the European Sovereign Debt Crisis prior to beginning my new job at Investcorp, an alternative investments firm best known for having acquired Gucci, Tiffany, and Saks Fifth Avenue. The timing was right to capitalize on the dislocations in the marketplace.

The research reports showed how the credit spreads of sovereign debt of Greece, Ireland, Italy, Portugal, and Spain had blown out, essentially meaning that the interest rates those countries had to pay had increased greatly. The corporate spreads had increased similarly by country.

It made me think about my days as an executive on Wall Street and how some large financial institutions might react during this sovereign debt crisis: pull all sovereign and corporate investments out of the affected country if that made sense holistically.

That would create forced sales.

On my first trip to the Gulf with Investcorp soon thereafter, I visited investors in Bahrain, Kuwait, the United Arab Emirates

(UAE), and Saudi Arabia. My arrival coincided with a violent period known as Arab Spring that began when a jobless student in Tunisia lit himself on fire when police did not allow him to operate his cart.

Violent protests had already led to the ousting of President Zine El Abidine Ben Ali of Tunisia who fled to Saudi Arabia, President Hosni Mubarak of Egypt who was detained in a military facility, and Colonel Muammar Gaddafi of Egypt who was cornered and killed. The successful ouster of long-standing regimes inspired a wave of violent protests in neighboring countries.

My first stop was to our Gulf headquarters in Manama, Bahrain. The clashes had begun earlier in the year with an anti-government "Day of Rage," and a protester was killed. Another was killed the next day when police clashed with the funeral procession. The protesters then camped out at Pearl Roundabout until police reclaimed the traffic circle, killing seven in the process. The Saudi government brought in over 1,000 troops. The UAE also sent in troops. Martial law was imposed. Global headlines ensued when F1 canceled their regularly scheduled race as a result.

Reading what felt like highly scripted government propaganda in the local paper in the Ritz Carlton looking out onto the placid Persian Gulf crystallized to me my new dynamic: Shi'ite protesters were trying to take out King Hamad bin Isa Al Khalifa and the 200-year-old dynasty, and the Royal Family was an investing client and Shaikh Mohamed Bin Isa Al Khalifa was on our board of directors.

In my first meeting with our Chairman, Nemir Kirdar, we discussed the opportunity to buy European companies with little or no exposure to the European economy that might be forced to sell. Nemir's office appeared identical to his offices in New York on Park Avenue and London. That was deliberate, as he employed the same architect to execute his desire—floor-to-ceiling wood paneling, beautiful collection of books and dignitaries, fireplace, gold-framed oil paintings, and Tiffany silver frames of family. Nemir was a man of few words. He listened intently for twenty minutes, saying nothing. His message was simple: "Let me know if I can help."

I had regular security briefs, including background checks on my drivers. Routes were chosen with the latest security information. Streets were blocked. Neighborhoods were off-limits. Thick black smoke was visible daily from the tire-burning protests.

Clearly, I didn't share with the head of security when I went to my Bahraini business school friend's house each time I was in town.

When I arrived at meetings with investors in their offices and homes, the Euro crisis wasn't lost on any of them. One of my meetings in Jeddah, Saudi Arabia, summed it up.

Jeddah is a port city directly across from Sudan in Africa on the Red Sea. The city has been settled for about 2,500 years and serves as the gateway for pilgrims journeying to Mecca. Coral buildings dating to the seventh century, 1,300 mosques, laws prohibiting buildings of other religions, hotel swimming pools and restaurants all separating men from women and children, alcohol prohibition, a parking lot that we drove by that serves as a weekly execution site—all contributed to a culture that felt like it was a long way from Bahrain or Dubai.

Upon showing my business card at the outset of our meeting, the centimillionaire investor proclaimed, "You are Europe? Buy nothing. I don't want to invest in anything in Europe."

To which I replied, "What if we found a company headquartered in Italy or Spain, that was growing in both revenues and profitability throughout the European Crisis, that had little or no exposure to the European economy, that typically would cost eight to ten times the multiple of their annual cash flows and that we were able to buy for three to four times their annual cash flows because they were forced to sell for some reason?"

"You bring me that company!" was the enthusiastic reply.

For the next year at our Grosvenor Street office building just off Grosvenor Square in Mayfair, London, I focused on identifying situations where there might be a need to sell off a business as a first lens of screening and prioritized the thinking in virtually all discussions with our investment professionals. Then, I went on a tear and hit the road. I had the audacity to engage whoever I thought could contribute to my prioritized mission and did my best to cover all angles of opportunity.

I met with prime ministers, CEOs, managing partners of dozens of private equity firms across Europe, and dozens of founders of businesses.

Within a year, we ended a three-year drought of acquisitions for Investcorp, Europe, and ended up buying five companies in two years, including Esmalglass, a company in Villarreal, Spain. Esmalglass had virtually no revenue exposure to Spain and little in Europe and had been growing revenue and profitability throughout the European Crisis. We acquired the company for under four times cash flow. Investcorp later sold the business for an extraordinary return.

The degree of variables in my day-to-day work relating to culture, language, economic volatility, social conscience, and regime change was high. Focus was an imperative.

Personal and professional, prioritize.

CHAPTER 25

WISDOM

ON MY FIRST VISIT to Buckingham Palace, my friend Tewodros Ashenafi, CEO of SouthWest Energy, and I spent most of the time giggling as we joked about the royal setting. The palace is 830,000 square feet of the most impeccably decorated and staffed interior environment on planet Earth. Admittedly, I was the troublemaker, not Tewodros.

"How do you like the royal peanuts?"

"Would it be inappropriate to take a royal paper napkin home?"

"Would the beefeater guards throw us in the royal dungeon for misbehavior?"

Next thing you know, we started wondering if our behavior was being noticed and if we were going to be thrown out of the palace. We had a very hard time stopping an awkward case of the giggles.

I mention Buckingham Palace, because like the White House, 10 Downing Street, or the C-suite offices of large multinational corporations and financial institutions, they scream success. And whatever that corner office or boss' room or principal's office that we think houses wisdom, the venue surrounding an individual certainly doesn't qualify their counsel.

Now, I've been fortunate to have been exposed to insanely successful people who had reputations of great wisdom like being on a board with Henry Kissinger or a fellow World Economic Forum Young Global Leader classmate with Sergey Brin and Larry Page. But I was never in a position to ask for their wisdom when it counted. Just because you're surrounded by people doesn't mean it does you any good when it matters. Further, that someone may be smart, experienced, or successful is only a qualifying element as it relates to the quality of their wisdom for you.

So who should you seek for counsel? Who will give you wisdom that matters to you?

Wisdom requires three elements.

First is having experiences that contribute and enrich the wisdom. Experiences provide the capacity for wisdom but do not assure it.

Second is the ability to tailor advice to suit the unique needs of the person seeking guidance.

Third, and most important in providing wisdom, is the capacity to care for the well-being of the advisee without reservation or bias or self-interest.

During one's lifetime, there will be few who provide selfless counsel. Virtually all the people who walk in and out of your life will have an agenda. My father taught me this by quoting his version of Miles's Law. "Tell me where you sit, and I'll tell you where you stand."

There will be no person on the Earth who will both understand you and selflessly counsel you better than your parents. For those of you who have parents with a breadth of experience, you are gifted with invaluable wisdom throughout your life. For those who have parents with limited experiences, you too will be gifted with the right boundaries in which to make your life decisions; they might just be a little wider.

In the summer of 1978, my parents had just told me it was time to go to the enclosed swimming pool area. They said let's stick together. Perhaps because I had just become a teenager earlier in the week in Nairobi, my thinking was that parental direction was no longer necessary.

I walked along a path from the main structure of the Samburu Game Lodge toward my wood and straw hut. Huts were spaced out every twenty yards or so on the right side of the path. On the left was a gradual slope of wild grass about ten yards wide that led down to the Ewaso Nyiro River. There were no fences to separate wildlife from tourists, just a couple signs that apparently sufficed. One sign read:

WILD ANIMALS ARE DANGEROUS!

THE LODGE ACCEPTS NO LIABILITY FOR
PERSONAL INJURY CAUSED BY WILD ANIMALS.

Another sign, just off the path before the slope to the river read:

DANGER, WILD ANIMALS!

On the reverse side, the sign read:

DANGER, HUMANS!

It was a hot day. Kenya is bordered by Uganda, Tanzania, Somalia, and the Indian Ocean. We were forty miles north of the equator on the border of the Samburu and Isiolo counties. No surprise, an elephant was cooling itself by the river.

I walked past a woman who was standing on the path with a small camera aimed at the elephant on the riverbank. Forty yards later, I glanced back and noticed that she had stepped off the path and was walking very slowly toward the elephant to get a closer picture. I stopped and watched. The woman proceeded to take one step closer when the elephant trumpeted to let everyone know it was game on.

The woman took two steps back and stumbled backward to the ground. The elephant turned around facing the woman and put his mass into drive up the slope. Out of nowhere, a Samburu savior ran and got in between her and the elephant waving his hands. The elephant ran up the hill to teach the Samburu savior his final lesson. Just before the elephant trampled him, the Samburu savior dove out of the way.

The sensational save by the Samburu savior was truly unforgettable. As was the fact that the elephant was now charging straight at me.

I quickly assessed the situation. Forty yards away from me was an African bush elephant (the official term is apparently, difficult to pronounce, *Loxodonta africana*). It is the largest living terrestrial animal with bulls reaching shoulder height of up to thirteen feet and a body weight of up to ten tons, or 20,000 pounds. I stood five feet tall weighing around 105 pounds. What I did not realize was that my challenger, *Loxodonta africana*, had a top speed of twenty-five miles per hour. Mine was about eight to ten miles per hour.

Run! I spun around and launched out of my starting blocks down the path away from the charging elephant. Running past a hut on my right, I glanced back at *Loxodonta africana* only to see he had been closing in rapidly. Run faster. As I approached another hut on my right, I took another glance over my shoulder at *Loxodonta africana*. He had now closed to within ten yards. He was going to catch me.

He had closed the distance that separated us so quickly; I knew that was the last glance over my shoulder I could afford. Instinctively, I took a right turn around the hut I was about to pass. Unfortunately, *Loxodonta africana* thought that was a pretty good idea too.

At this point, I didn't know exactly how close *Loxodonta africana* was to teaching me the lesson that he really wanted to teach the woman taking his picture at the riverbank but knew that there was no chance of escape by running straight. I figured taking another right turn around the back of the hut. If he followed me, he'd catch me. If he didn't, I'd escape. Fortunately, this time, *Loxodonta africana* charged straight on.

I continued to circle the hut in a panic, only satisfied that I'd live to see another day when I saw *Loxodonta africana* in the distance after having run all the way around the hut.

There's a poem in French about fathers that comes close to encapsulating how valuable a parent's wisdom is and how too many people waste too much time before they figure it out. It goes something like this:

At 6 years old: Dad knows everything

At 10 years old: Dad knows a lot of things

At 15 years old: I know as much as Dad

At 18 years old: Decidedly, Dad doesn't know much

At 30 years old: We could at least ask Dad's opinion

At 40 years old: Dad, at least, knows something

At 50 years old: Dad's right

At 60 years old: Ah! If only we still had Dad around to ask

Parents are biologically coded with wisdom for their children. Use it.

C H A P T E R   2 6

GIVING

I ARRIVED AT JFK AIRPORT in New York via Aspen for my first pilgrimage to Lourdes in France with the Sovereign Military Hospitaller Order of Saint John of Jerusalem, of Rhodes, and of Malta. The Order of Malta or Knights of Malta, founded in 1048, is a Catholic lay religious order that is the oldest surviving institution in western civilization. Its history is a deep dive into the history of Europe and Catholicism.

Annually, we take malades (many terminally ill patients) to Lourdes to experience a miracle or grace in their last days on Earth. The highlight of the pilgrimage is to bathe in the waters at the Grotto of Massabielle where the Immaculate Virgin Mary appeared to St. Bernadette eighteen times in 1858. There, on February 25, 1858, the Blessed Virgin Mary instructed St. Bernadette to dig in the dirt to create a water spring and to "drink at the spring and bathe in it." Over 200 million people have visited.

As I joined our group of a couple hundred people in our military uniforms, I was approached by one of the organizers. He said, "Let me introduce you to your malade." I joyfully greeted my malade, a septuagenarian with advanced Parkinson's disease, and extended my hand.

He didn't look at me. After making a few cheerful comments and attempts at conversation starters that elicited no reply, the organizer pulled me aside and informed me that he wanted me to engage with one of the tougher personality assignments on my first trip.

For the next week, my life was that of charioteer, pulling the chariot of my malade from event to event around Lourdes. The process to travel to spiritual events is called a procession, a military exercise in formation. However, at the end of events immediately preceding lunch and dinner, charioteers, malades, their caregivers, and the other knights, dames, and volunteers are free to proceed to the hotel bases as they wish. I decided that was my opportunity.

I decided to pull my malade through the hundreds of chariots on the skinny streets of Lourdes using the best of what I had learned at Skip Barber Racing in Laguna Seca. Every trek back to the hotel was a race to have my malade be the first at a meal. Strategy was key, and much like approaching a toll booth that has extensive lines, the lane choice was critical. After the first two speed sessions, my malade grumbled, "Did they send you to me to kill me?" He was soon looking forward to each "race" with great anticipation.

On the day before departure back to the United States, we were all given a day off. I suggested to him that it might be cool to ascend to the Château Fort de Lourdes if he didn't need the time off. The Chateau dates to Roman times but was captured by Charlemagne in the eighth century. In 1590, it was a royal domain for Henri IV. In the seventeenth and eighteenth centuries, it was transformed into a prison and was known as the Bastille of the Pyrenees. It stands atop a rock peak in the Seven Valleys and towers over the town of Lourdes. He looked at me, "You think we can make it?" My honesty prevailed. "I don't know, but if we don't, it could be pretty bad." He responded, "Let's go! If I'm gonna go, that's the way to go."

The trip from the Hotel Mediterranee where we were staying was only 1.1 kilometers to the top. I had my hands gripped to the pull bar behind me that was carrying my malade in the three-wheeled chariot. How hard could that be? The last few hundred meters are very steep. If my hands let go, he was in for a backward ride down the steep access road. Just put one foot in front of the other. The Jacobs Ladder in the gym had nothing on this. At one point, I went to put one foot in front of the other and failed to advance my foot. Instead, I lost my forward-leaning balance and had to spin around temporarily only holding the chariot with one hand to grab the handle with both hands facing downhill.

"Maybe we should turn around." I suggested with sweat dripping visibly down my face. "Not a chance," he replied.

Upon our triumphant arrival at the Chateau Fort, my malade poured out his hopes, his fears, his life, his love. We spent close to two hours talking about things that matter. Our backgrounds could not have been more different. Our most closely held priorities could not have been more similar.

I planned on a pilgrimage to Lourdes in service of the sick. I went and continue to go for enrichment. The pilgrimages have taught me how to better give that gift to my children. Every time we leave the house is an opportunity—whether near or far.

Most recently, I took my sons Alexander and Leo to the 2021 US Olympic Trials and 2022 World Championships for track and field in Eugene, Oregon. While the sport was memorable, their most vivid memories were our daily trips to visit one of the many parks populated with homeless people. We walked and talked to as many as we could. For most, we were able to thank them for the service they had extended to our communities at some point during their lives.

Like many encounters, it heightened my sense of immediacy to get more done because I owe a lot more. To me, it's a race against time to ensure that I provide the return on the talent given to me and the privileges afforded to me. I'm way behind but thankful that there's still time.

On a completely different scale, I was on stage in the auditorium of the 2.3 million square foot campus of Sears Holdings in Hoffman Estates, Illinois, with one of my heroes, Johann Olav Koss.

Johann is a soft-spoken, impossibly humble, yet majestically built 6'2" Olympic gold medalist and world record–setting speed skater from Norway.

Johann had just flown in from Canada to talk in a speaker series for our roughly 300,000 employees where they heard and engaged with extraordinary people.

Johann described how immediately prior to the Olympic games in his home country in Lillehammer, Norway, he visited Eritrea in Africa. He described his sheltered life and how the trip changed him forever through his exposure to the ravages of war and poverty on children.

On this trip, he asked a young boy why he was so popular, and the boy said because he had a long-sleeved shirt. When Johann asked him to explain why that was so important, he was taken aback when the boy replied that he could tie the sleeves of the shirt to bundle it and use it as a soccer ball. They had no balls to play. Johann internalized the injustice and dedicated himself to making a difference.

Every Sears and Kmart employee in attendance could feel his sincerity.

On February 12, 1994, to the roar of over 10,000 spectators and a sea of Norwegian waving flags jammed in Hamar Olympic Hall, also known as the Viking Ship, Johann bested forty-four competitors from seventeen countries to take the gold medal in the 1,500-meter-speed skating race, breaking the world record.

On February 13, 1994, again in the Viking Ship, Johann bested thirty-two competitors from seventeen countries to take the gold medal in the 5,000 meter, again breaking the world record.

On February 20, 1994, again in the Viking Ship, Johann bested sixteen competitors from ten countries to take the gold medal in the 10,000 meter, again breaking the world record.

Johann described the jubilation. A television cameraman and reporter interrupted the celebration and stumped him, extending the microphone toward his face saying, "Johann. Three Olympic gold medals. Three world records. You have given Norwegians' joy. You have made our country proud. What would you like to tell your fellow countrymen?"

Johann said that amid the physical and mental exhaustion that accompanies fulfilling a lifelong pursuit, he could only think of one thing. The children of Eritrea. He was given an opportunity. They weren't.

As his mind raced to think of what to say, he decided to just speak from his heart even though he didn't know what was going to come out on live television in front of millions.

Johann recollected replying, "If my effort gave you any pride or joy, then please commit to giving $5 to a foundation that I will create to give the children in Africa equipment to play sport. They have a right to play."

The outpouring of support launched Right to Play. Today, the humanitarian effort has impacted over two million children in seventeen countries.

Rewards from giving always outweigh whatever was given.

LISTENING

THE BUSTLE OF eight adults and nine children all gathered at my parents' house in Florida for the Christmas holidays made for a chaotic environment. Emailing on my phone sitting at the breakfast table in the kitchen ensured my ability to engage with everyone episodically as they made pit stops for a bite to eat or drink.

The kitchen table was loaded with Christmas snacks. At the center of the table was a glorious untouched cheese platter that had just been delivered to my parents as a seasonal gift from one of their friends, a mountain of cubes of cheese—Mount Christmas. The top few cheese cubes were particularly colorful as they were laced with hot green and red peppers.

Louis, my three-year-old nephew, bounded into the kitchen. He surveyed the room for the most delicious edible. He scanned and passed on the array of seasonal nuts, popcorns, fruit baskets, cakes, and cookies. His eyes locked on to Mount Christmas. A hypnotic state of focus ensued.

I put my phone down and watched him climb onto a chair, reach out, and grab the peppered cheese disguised as a candied treat on top of Mount Christmas. He stuck it in his mouth and chewed the greatest prize in the kitchen.

The joy of winning the lottery plastered on his face was quickly replaced with a mask of horror, betrayal, and disgust. The three-year-old instantaneously assessed extraction alternatives and stood up on the chair. He leaned directly over the top of Mount Christmas and proceeded to spit out the masticated cheese cube in a horrifying saliva wrapping to its rightful place atop Mount Christmas. He exclaimed his disgust and proceeded to sprint out of the kitchen of betrayal.

I had barely picked up my phone to re-engage with my emails when my eighty-year-old famished father entered the kitchen for a pit stop of delight. His eyes, precisely like his grandson Louis, surveyed the room for the most delicious edible. He scanned and passed on the array of seasonal nuts, popcorns, fruit baskets, cakes, and cookies. His eyes locked on to Mount Christmas. A hypnotic state of focus ensued.

Throughout my life, my parents have protected me. Frankly, had my listening skills been honed earlier in life, I'd surely be in a better place. Fortunately, as an adult, there have been moments where I've been able to reciprocate. This was unquestionably one of those moments. Immediately, I intervened to protect my father.

"Pops," I said.

My father had served in the navy. His hypnotic state was much like the onboard Airborne Interception radar on a naval fighter jet when it picks up a target and feeds the information to the onboard weapon systems. As we all know, when the target is within the kill range of a particular system, it is fired and guided on to the target until impact. My Pops was locked in and closing in on Mount Christmas.

"Pops," I repeated.

He wasn't listening. He reached the table. His arm extended with great precision to the top of Mount Christmas.

"Pops!" I yelled.

Target hit. Target destroyed, as he placed the three-year-old's saliva-wrapped masticated peppered cheese into his mouth.

"What?" he replied.

After having reviewed with him the chronology of events immediately preceding his kitchen entrance, the glow of joy of having secured the greatest prize of the kitchen was replaced with a now familiar mask of horror, betrayal, and disgust.

IN A DIFFERENT PLACE AND TIME, I was taking a gondola ride up Aspen Mountain with a well-known investor friend, and we were talking about marathon running. I described one of my races. It was a distance relay called the Hood to Coast in Oregon. I said it was something like a 195-mile race that we started at midnight near the top of Mount Hood and ended up on the beach the next day around six o'clock in the evening because the sun had just set. Without a second of hesitation, he said, "That's impossible—that's a 5 minute 32 second per mile pace." I checked the math later; he was right. As it turns out, the sun sets around eight o'clock that time of year, so if I assume it was an hour after sunset, that would be a 6 minute 28 second pace; that sounds right. We were a fast team, but we weren't Alberto Salazar fast; he was a well-known Nike athlete and marathon runner that flew by me on my first leg. I never met anyone who could compute like my friend—not even close.

That being said, he is so sharp and thinks things through so deeply, listening is at times a challenge for him.

Another friend of mine is a venture capitalist. He told me about a new company he was involved with and said that my friend should use their services for one of the companies that he had invested in. The fit seemed logical. I told the venture capitalist that if I engaged my friend and they used this company's product, they would want equity in the company in return for having used the services as it would make the company more valuable considering its early stage of development. He said they could have 10 percent of the equity if they used it.

I then called my investor friend, and he quickly cut me off. He had studied his investment in this company and had little patience for anything he hadn't previously thought about.

Not long after, the company I referred to him filed for an initial public offering (IPO) valued at $11 billion. The stock traded up to about $15 billion shortly thereafter. Even two years later, it had a market cap exceeding $7 billion. No matter how you slice it, it was about a $1 billion listening mistake.

The reason I chose this particular investor friend to make the point of the importance of listening is to establish that no matter how great your brain may be, how successful you may be, or how wealthy you may be—and my friend ticked all the boxes sensationally—you'd be better off if you were a great listener. It's hard. He is someone who can get away with not listening at times. He's that smart, and he works that hard.

When I applied to colleges, there was a standard essay question something along the lines of "What's your biggest weakness?" My reply was, "I have a hard time being open to others' ideas after I have already thought carefully about the topic."

Assuming the person who you are listening to knows things, or has a perspective you don't, is a pretty good place to start.

Being a better listener is a lifelong pursuit.

CHAPTER 28

COMMUNICATING

I HAD BEEN FRIENDS for a while with a controversial founder of a large hedge fund. My family was invited to share Thanksgiving dinner at his home. I gave him a hug as an initial greeting at the door (he's not a big hugger), and my brother, sister, and parents followed in.

My septuagenarian mother—the matriarch of our family—was a queen of philanthropy in Chicago and master of pleasantries. She launched into a spontaneous gracious doorstep thank you speech for having us over for the holiday dinner.

"It is so nice to finally meet you. A day of thanksgiving ... that I, as a mother, may celebrate in thanksgiving for the relationship that you and my son have cultivated. And that we may build on that friendship to share and extend together is all the more reason to give thanks." The doorstep speech continued for a full two minutes. With no preparation, my mother delivered a speech worthy of a high-profile gala dinner. I am pretty sure she worked in a quote from Mother Teresa. Her address concluded with a deliberate and poignant "I know Scott thanks you—our family thanks you—I thank you."

Throughout the entire address, he was silent, looking at her.

Upon conclusion, he simply said, "Don't thank me. I didn't invite you."

My mother reacted as if she had been sprayed in the face by bear repellant on the sunny holiday. Unfortunately, my friend's wife wasn't present to clean up the social oil spill. She is a most elegant woman who seamlessly builds bridges of understanding with grace and a most gentle touch.

He said, "Don't thank me. I didn't invite you." Why would he say that? Knowing him well, I'm pretty sure it was because it was his wife's idea to have our families celebrate Thanksgiving together, and it would be inappropriate for him to accept this wonderful gratitude from my mother when it was she who was the rightful recipient of these kind words.

If you bring your own communication framework (admittedly, even a generally practiced one), my friend's message would have been misinterpreted as "I don't want you here," which could not have been further from the truth.

At the age of five, we moved from Deerfield, Illinois, to São Paulo, Brazil. On the plane ride, my globally astute father told us not to use the "OK" hand sign. He said that in the United States, the OK sign is a hand gesture form of communication, meaning everything is fine or that you agree with someone. In Brazil, it's like showing someone the middle finger.

When I recently came home from a trip and gave each of my two sons a Matchbox toy car, my eldest, Alexander, said, "My car's faster than Leo's car, right?" He wasn't asking me which car was faster. He was asking me if I loved him more, and he wanted affirmation that his toy was a little bit better than his brother's.

When talking to a British CEO while working in London, he told me, "That's most interesting." He was actually saying, "Dumbest idea ever." Similarly, when our French national head of European corporate investments at Investcorp said, "It's complicated," he was actually telling me, "Dumbest idea ever."

Communication differences are grounded in varying geographic, social, and cultural foundations. Words and body language matter, but context does too.

Focus on the intent of communication to understand the message.

MATERIALISM

WE HAD JUST CELEBRATED my fifty-second birthday the prior week, and we were walking along the River Seine from Ile Saint Louis to the Cathedrale Notre Dame de Paris. For my birthday, Isabelle had gifted to me a tour of the Cathedrale with its rector, Monsignor Patrick Chauvet.

Even though I had lived in Paris for five years in my formative years, had been back annually for thirty years, had all three of our children baptized at the Cathedrale and it was our parish when staying in Paris, for whatever reason, I had never visited the crypt or the bell towers. I was very excited.

Upon arrival at the rectory, Monsignor Chauvet greeted us and apologized for being unable to show us the crypt or the tower because those were operated by the French government. He said he hoped we would enjoy what he was allowed to show us which were some areas not open to the public.

We visited an enclosed prayer garden for the priests, climbed to the balcony level overlooking the inside of the church, and walked on the balcony on the outside of the church. All the while, Monsignor

Chauvet fascinated us with the 850-plus-year history, pointing out hidden elements in plain sight. After an hour, he said that was all he had planned except one last thing he'd like to show us, the Crown of Thorns. I was stunned.

Isabelle asked Monsignor Chauvet to kindly explain the history. He gladly obliged. Following Jesus' crucifixion, the Crown of Thorns had been in Jerusalem and Constantinople, for protection during invasions. In 1239, King Louis of France saw an opportunity to secure the most prized relic in the world in light of Emperor Baldwin, the Broke of Constantinople's, desperate need for finances. King Louis was flush with gold. He gave the emperor all his gold and further indebted France but negotiated to secure the relic. In preparation for the arrival of the relic, King Louis fasted. In August, 778 years ago, King Louis ordered the emperor's seal on the silver coffer to be broken and the gold box inside to be opened. King Louis was overwhelmed.

King Louis then built one of the most beautiful chapels in the world, La Sainte Chapelle on Ile de la Cite nearby, to serve as the most extraordinary reliquary. In the French Revolution, La Sainte Chapelle was taken over, and the Crown of Thorns made its way back to the Cathedrale where it has been since. Monsignor Chauvet said that most recently, he had brought it out for Melania Trump, who cried with emotion as did Vladimir Putin.

The Crown of Thorns was brought out from the multilayered security system. Monsignor opened the red velvet box and removed the relic. It was difficult to process two millennia at the same time because of the significance of the relic. My sons and I prayed.

In my childhood, possessions were primarily a source of entertainment. And of all my possessions, my blankie stood alone atop all of them for a decade—just as my son, Alexander, has his blankie; my son, Leopold, has his ducky; and my daughter, Anastasia, has her unicorn.

My blankie was a vehicle that transported me to a safe place. The consistency of safe moments with blankie continued to reinforce its magical powers of comfort. When bullied, punished, a disappointment or failure to loved ones, blankie was always there providing a comforting place. Blankie has been in storage for over five decades. The possession was irrelevant. However, a child having a safe place is incredibly important. The possession was a conduit.

In my adolescence, possessions were academic and recreational instruments. Soccer cleats, running shoes, an Apple llc. There were moments of joy receiving various possessions, but in retrospect, the joy was more about knowing that someone loved me. Reflecting on which ones mattered the most to me, still in my possession are coins blessed by Saint Pope John Paul II from when I met him in the Vatican. The possessions have no intrinsic value, yet they are my most prized for what they signify. They represent my desire to be close to the Saint. Again, the possession was only a conduit to something that matters in my life.

In my twenties, life was about athletics. Successes were memorialized with medals, trophies, and game balls. They help relive the moment and rekindle a confidence to go boldly in the face of whatever challenges may come my way. The possessions are worthless, yet they are a reminder of what it takes to break new ground.

In my thirties, there was an exhilaration associated with buying a house or a car. The feeling was always fleeting. The possessions were a conduit to feeling a sense of delivering on the expectations of my father.

In my forties, my prized possessions were news clippings and corporate and civic awards. My father and brother had established benchmarks of achievement. My father had been vice chairman of Booz Allen & Hamilton and CEO of two public companies, including Chiquita, the banana company. My brother founded a credit opportunity hedge fund. Each memento that met that standard in my mind became a favorite possession. Again, each was materially worthless but transported me to a feeling or place of perceived arrival.

In my fifties, I can afford and enjoy nice things because hard work paid off, but I can't think of any possessions that really matter. In my life I coveted things but was always left empty. Giving is actually much more satisfying.

As the decades pass
through the hourglass of life,
it becomes increasingly clear
that most possessions matter little;
they always were and always will be conduits
to the things that really matter in life.

CHAPTER 30

SERVICE

MOST OF US KNOW or have heard stories of those who serve that humble us. For decades, the stories of a colonel in the US Army remain with me as one shining and inspirational example.

Colonel Jon Vanden Bosch graduated near the top of his class at West Point and had attended Airborne and Ranger Schools, the US Army Command and General Staff College, the US Army War College, and the Foreign Service Institute. He had command postings in Europe, Korea, and Vietnam. He served for a year on the ground in Vietnam where 58,148 Americans were killed and 75,000 severely disabled.

Among his honors, he was awarded the Air Medal, Combat Infantry Badge, Meritorious Service Medal, Bronze Star with Oak Leaf Cluster, Parachute Badge, Legion of Merit, Joint Service Commendation Medal, Vietnam Service Medal, Republic of Vietnam Civil Action Medal First Class, Vietnam Gallantry Cross, Republic of Vietnam Armed Forces Medal First Class, Vietnam Gallantry Cross, and Army Commendation Medal.

General Westmoreland, who he served with and for which I have a cherished picture of them together in Vietnam, wrote to him telling him he was one of "the most highly qualified officers."

Even upon concluding his service in Vietnam where he was advising the province chief in his negotiations with the North Vietnamese team, he insisted that he be the last to leave notwithstanding his rank. Tragically, he had one more horror to endure as he watched the second to last helicopter get shot down with his fellow servicemen—a burden for his honor that he carried throughout his life.

On September 21, 2016, we buried Jon at Arlington National Cemetery. We followed the long military procession through the cemetery walking behind the lone charger, a saddled horse with no rider, and a pair of boots set backward in the stirrups, signifying that a warrior has fallen in battle and a poignant reminder of the sacrifices so many Americans have made for our freedoms.

President George W. Bush said, "Laura and I are honored to salute the service of Jon and pay tribute to his life. Jon was a good man who devoted his career to serving his fellow Americans … and worked hard to make a difference. I am grateful for his contributions to Houston, to the Lone Star State, and to our Nation."

Colonel Jon Vanden Bosch was my uncle and godfather.

In the summer of 2019, our family traveled to Normandy, France, for the seventy-fifth anniversary of the landings on D-Day to educate our children.

We began this service transmission to our next generation of family members at Arromanches-les-Bains in the Calvados region of Normandy in northwest France. Located at the center of Gold Beach, it was the site of one of two ports constructed to enable the disembarkation of 2.5 million men, a half million vehicles, and over 100,000 tons of supplies in the first hundred days.

We visited Omaha Beach where 2,400 allies were killed by the German 352nd Division.

We paid our respects at the American Cemetery and Memorial in Colleville-sur-Mer, among the hundreds of rows of crosses as far as the eye can see, where 9,388 Americans who were killed in World War II are buried.

Democracy comes at a cost. Freedom comes at a cost. Life, liberty, and the pursuit of happiness come at a cost.

Those who serve are the first to raise their hands to protect the freedoms which we cherish.

Do not let others' disrespect, divisiveness, and negativity toward our country impair your efforts to make a positive difference. Our forefathers created a blueprint for independence and democracy in the Declaration of Independence and the Constitution of the United States, which is the envy of people around the world.

Make a positive difference for your fellow citizens. Make a positive difference for your community. Make a positive difference for your country.

We can't all be war heroes. We can all serve.

RELENTLESSNESS

MY BROTHER AND I took our seats in the recently renovated Estadi Olimpic de Montjuic in Barcelona twenty or so rows up from the finish line. Eight athletes loosened up and got set in their starting blocks. In lane 3 was the reigning Olympic champion Steve Lewis from the United States, in lane 4 was Cuban record holder Roberto Hernandez, and in lane 5 was Derek Redmond from the United Kingdom, the British record holder. This was the first semifinals of the men's 400-meter race at the 1992 Olympic Games. Our eyes are on the three athletes in the middle lanes.

Bang! They blast out of their starting blocks and in no time are around the first bend. Halfway down the back stretch, one runner starts limping and grabbing his hamstring. I couldn't tell from my seat who it was. Seven men are left sprinting around the far side of the track. They're making their way to the last 100 meters. Here they come. Lewis wins it in 44.50 seconds, about 0.6 seconds off Olympic record pace, and Hernandez is second. Team USA is in the finals.

On the far side of the track, Derek Redmond, who was the one who was injured, waves off the attendants who looked like they were going to escort him off the track to make way for the next race. He starts hopping on his left foot. It looks like he wants to finish the race. This is going to take a while. A minute goes by as he's still hopping. He's slowly, and clearly painfully, making his way around the bend. We stand to clap for him. We're not sure he's going to make it by the look and slowing pace. I stick my fingers in my mouth and whistle as loudly as possible.

With about 100 meters to go, it looks like a fan is running at him. Attendants attempt to stop him, but he insists. We assume that's got to be his father. It is. Derek puts his arm around his dad and covers his face of anguish and tears. They stopped. It looks like it is over. Attendants looked like they wanted them off the track. Derek's dad tells the attendant to go away. Derek and his dad started to walk again. Derek's face is buried in his father's chest, and his Dad guides them to the finish line.

Just about everyone is standing in the stadium by then. Everyone is cheering, clapping, whistling.

With every step, Derek's body unleashes new higher doses of pain and punishment. With every step, Derek's body contributes less and his father more. With every step, all of us in the stadium cheered, clapped, and whistled louder and louder wanting to support their battle against Derek's pain.

Derek Redmond and his father crossed the finish line to the loudest roar of the 1992 Olympic Games. Derek finishes what he started.

Derek later said,

> Whatever your dream is in life—it could be something quite small, it could be something absolutely huge—you have to have 100 percent belief and confidence you can achieve that goal.

If you don't have that belief, that passion that you can achieve this, I would suggest you are chasing the wrong dream.

Invariably, persevering is a prerequisite for success. Challenges and failure are omnipresent. Eddie Lampert, my boss at Sears Holdings who was the then majority owner and chairman and is off-the-charts smart, gave me a thoughtful perspective: "You only really get to learn who a person is when things are going against them."

Unlike my prior experiences, working at CDI Corp was a steep turnaround project; the stock had been on a steady decline. I put my money where my mouth was by constructing a compensation package that included below market salary and bonus amounts yet large payouts if we could double or triple the stock price.

CDI was a company with acute client concentration in each of its dozen businesses (three clients accounted for 75 percent of revenues for our average business) and with business concentration in commoditized temporary staff in the oil and gas sector. Upon my arrival, the price of oil proceeded to drop from $97 per barrel to under $40. Three-quarters of our clients experienced significant revenue declines themselves. Many immediately responded by cutting their temporary staff (our core business).

To make matters worse, our company had previously cut its revenue-generating capacity as part of continuous cost cutting, and, as a result, there was no revenue-generating capacity to replenish the lost business. Most businesses, including our largest, didn't have a single business development person. In fact, the stated strategy in the annual report prior to my arrival was "to maintain clients." Well, we maintained clients, and our financial performance and stock price suffered painfully.

By leveraging the talents of the existing team and the best minds we could attract to CDI Corp., together, we created a strategy I believed could work. First, we would sell every one of the dozen businesses that had been commoditized over decades. Concurrently, we would acquire IT staffing and solutions companies which provided desperately needed technology talent to a corporate world undergoing disruption and disintermediation due to new business models emerging from rapid technological change.

The board approved the plan to recast the portfolio including our first recommended acquisition. However, the board declined to approve our first recommended disposition and put a moratorium on any dispositions wanting to focus on running the existing portfolio of businesses.

For two years, the team had worked as hard as teams compensated ten times more. Long hours and weekends pouring over research, creating analytics, firing poor performers, bringing on great performers, and executing as one, the team delivered. While we had saved every client relationship delivering a 99.5 percent request for proposal re-compete success rate, drove operating expenses to the lowest level in twenty-five years, stabilized revenues, delivered an annualized cash flow turnaround of $15 million in our most recent quarter, and were rated a "strong buy" by the equity research analyst covering our stock, having studied the company, I saw no viable organic path forward. If you believe the direction you're being told to drive is destined to fail, you probably shouldn't be the driver.

I resigned amicably, handing the board a most qualified team, including Michael Castleman (former co-head of a venture capital business and now chief growth and transformation officer at Witt-

Kieffer), Hugo Malan (formerly McKinsey & Co. and subsequently president of two large staffing organizations), and Jill Albrinck (formerly partner at Booz Allen Hamilton and now CEO at MVM Growth Partners).

Lots of consulting work later after I left, the company was subjected to the outcome we had previously communicated as most likely: selling off the pieces.

I was now unemployed and had virtually no capital. That is a completely unsettling and inescapable feeling. It was extraordinarily stressful. My family obligations had continuous expenses draining my bank account, and nothing was coming in.

Frankly, part of me just couldn't bear to see anyone, so I had to get out of town. We sold our house in Villanova, Pennsylvania, and the family took the opportunity to stay in Paris for several months. Every day, I walked my sons to the French public school on Rue Poulletier on Isle Saint Louis and then randomly paced the streets of Paris trying to walk off my stress and consider options. Clouds of failure and stress followed me everywhere.

Following my non-compete agreement, I got to work.

The most important missing piece was capital. Mike Odrich was a former colleague of mine on Wall Street. I had learned a ton from Mike. He had created a $40 billion private equity business from scratch and was one of the most talented among our 30,000 employees. The choice of capital partner was the most important thing I did.

A&M Capital embraced the idea. I trusted Mike completely, having witnessed him for well over a decade as ethical beyond reproach. No surprise, the partners he selected for the project, Alex Nivelle and Todd Rubin, were smart as can be and hardworking and cut from the same "do the right thing" cloth.

Within two years of our first acquisition, we had bought eight IT staffing companies and sold the company, ettain group, to Manpower for $925 million. We made over $1/2 billion profit for our investors on a little under $140 million of equity investment—a multiple on invested capital of 3.3× or over 100 percent annual rate of return in two years.

Be relentless in the pursuit of your destination. Believe in yourself even when the lights go out.

The will to ascend, more than anything else, will define how high the peak.

CHAPTER 32

FAITH

ON JUNE 10, 2019, I woke up at six o'clock in the morning at the American Inn Hotel in Cañon City, a small town in south central Colorado. My room in the motel featured a direct view into the grill of a parked pick up truck. I was pretty sore from the past two days of biking.

On June 11, I was due to deliver a speech to a number of presidents of various US Olympic sports programs, such as USA Swimming, USA Track & Field, and others at the US Olympic Training Center in Colorado Springs, Colorado. I had agreed to talk about innovation.

I had the genius idea that I needed to connect with the audience on athletics. I decided to bike to my speech as it would somehow come up as a "Just Do It" kind of moment despite the fact that I hadn't ridden a bicycle in two years and was woefully out of shape.

The trip was 203 miles with over 12,000 feet of vertical climb. Google Maps said that was twenty-one hours of biking, so I allowed for a three-day ride.

I hopped on my bike and made my way east down Royal George Boulevard, also known as US 50 East. I enjoyed passing through towns I had never been to before. Only five miles away was the Supermax prison in Florence. Known as the Alcatraz of the Rockies, this prison houses the worst of the worst. Zacarias Moussaoui of 9/11, who almost got me, and Ramzi Yousef and Mahmud Abouhalima from the 1993 WTC bombings, who also almost got me, were imprisoned there. There were many other super villains there. I thought about adding the five miles to and from to see what their sentence looked like, but I didn't want the distraction of negativity. Ride on.

I made my way over to the Waffle Wagon across the street and did my best to eat something that would get me through my bike ride. I ordered a delicious grilled ham and cheese sandwich and a coffee. I admired the place and envied the people.

I hopped back on the bike and headed east. At the intersection of US 50 and Colorado 115 North (also known as the Vietnam Veterans Memorial Highway), I rode up the exit off ramp and took a left onto the highway that would lead me to Colorado Springs. The roads were starting to pick up morning traffic.

Ten or so miles up the highway, I had just finished a climb and was about to enjoy another descent. I watched my speed. Time to destination was irrelevant. When I hit 30 mph, I stopped pedaling. The amount of debris on the shoulder was becoming a concern. I weaved left and right avoiding visible stones and was increasingly conscious of the vibration caused by smaller pebbles on the shoulder.

It was a two-lane 60 mph speed limit highway at this point. I peered over my left shoulder and saw that there were no vehicles coming down the hill headed north as I was. There was a rumble strip on the shoulder. I had passed over a few on the trip and deduced that at 30 mph, I had the speed to maintain a straight line.

As I leaned to my left to get on the highway, my front wheel wobbled. The bike was heading left into the highway, but the wobbling increased right, left, right. Eject.

I was thrown over the bars of the bike. At this point, I was in the middle of the northbound lane with my weight and momentum carrying me further left into oncoming traffic. I had no clip in shoes, so my body projected forward with no resistance. I was in the air headed straight at a white truck in the oncoming lane headed south.

For a moment, I thought about how stupid I had been to cross the rumble strip. It was an unknown, at minimum an untested risk. Why hadn't I just slowed my bike down? Why didn't I stop and regroup? Why didn't I bike slowly down the highway hill shoulder? But I didn't waste too much time beating myself up while heading toward oncoming traffic. I was traveling 30 mph—they were traveling 70 mph. Trucks always win contests with human projectiles.

The mental math kicked in mid-flight. Was there anything I could do to improve my chances of survival? No. The math was clear to me. There was no chance for survival. There were multiple vehicles heading right at me led by the white truck. There was no way for me to change my trajectory into their lane. We were close enough to each other that there was no chance for them to change their course.

I was not afraid. I did not fear the pain. I knew there was an inevitable course of action that was underway. I surrendered myself to the inevitable. I hit the pavement close to the middle of the north- and southbound lanes. What I saw next was an indecipherable series of photo stills akin to YouTube videos posted of skiers with GoPro cameras on their helmets falling at high speeds and tumbling. Flashes of hundreds of images processed and developed too fast for my mind to synthesize clearly.

My midair calculation had me hitting directly in the middle of the white truck. The hundreds of images were unclear. As I rolled along the asphalt into oncoming traffic, I fully expected the lights to simply go out. When I knew I hadn't been hit by the grill of the truck,

I expected to be run over by a wheel or hit by the undercarriage of the truck or a following car. I did not anticipate pain, just lights going out.

Whatever was next for me was where I was headed. I thought about my wife, Isabelle, and my kids, Alexander, Leopold, and Anastasia. They would have enough financial resources to have a wonderful life, but I worried about the impact of my death on my children.

I knew that this moment was now about me and God; I let them go. It's a very individual moment in time when you know you are going to pass on. I placed my faith in Him. I wasn't begging or praying. I knew that whatever life I had lived had already run its course. I was now embarking on the next phase of existence.

I had lots of close calls in my life, many I have not shared in this book. All of those seemed minor because right now was the only time when I was certain this existence was over. Yet, I was at peace with that. I continued to tumble.

At some point, I opened my eyes and lifted my head. I was alive.

I was in the middle of the highway of oncoming traffic. I had to get to the side of the road. I saw a man standing on the shoulder and yelled, "Call 911!" I hadn't processed how the man got there, but in retrospect, I must have blacked out for a period of time for him to have pulled his car over to the side of the road and gotten out. How long was I out? I didn't know. I just knew I had to get off the highway. Somehow, I survived and had to get to safety. As I lifted my body, my right side hurt. As it turned out, it was a fractured pelvic bone. I limped to the shoulder of the northbound lane and lay down.

Within moments, two civilians presented themselves as nurses and began talking to me and comforting me. I had seen the concussion protocol many times, and their actions were part of it. However, I had no idea what shape I was in. Clearly, I was in shock, and that helped me deal with whatever pain I had. Every extremity of my body began stinging. I was cut everywhere. Their questions were relentless. I just wanted to fall asleep. I was tired from three days and 190 miles of biking.

I asked the nurses how I looked. They just said I had a bad fall and asked if I wanted them to call someone. That didn't sound good.

"What year is it?"

"What is your name?"

"When were you born?"

"Who is president of the United States?"

I was being bombarded with questions.

Someone said they found my cell phone a hundred feet up the highway. The nurse dialed for me, and I spoke to my wife, Isabelle, after the nurse had given her a summary of what had happened. I recall it going something like this:

Isabelle: "How are you?"

Me: "I don't know."

Isabelle: "What happened?"

Me: "I crashed."

Isabelle: "Are you OK—what hurts?"

Me: "I don't know—I can't tell what happened, and I don't know how bad it is. Find out where I'm going, and please meet me there."

Isabelle: "Let me speak to the nurse again."

A series of civil and first responders joined the assessment. A firefighter was cutting all my clothes off with scissors. I overheard:

"Did anyone see if a vehicle hit him?"

"Yes, it was that car over there."

"When is the ambulance coming?"

"We don't have time for an ambulance—we need him airlifted."

"Where are we taking him?"

"We need him at the trauma center *now*."

They wrapped me in an air-filled neck and back brace and placed me on a gurney. A tripod tube was inserted into my left arm vein. I was at the mercy of the competence and care of the first responders and once again owed them a debt of gratitude.

I recited the Our Father and Hail Mary. I was preparing for whatever was next for me. I surrendered to Him, again.

The propellers of the helicopter created a rush of wind as it landed on the highway. The responders warned me that once I was in the care of the trauma center, they'd do lots of "things" to me. At this point, I was in no position to have a view. They hoisted my gurney onto the helicopter. The medical attendant administered fentanyl. Having seen a *60 Minutes* television episode on the power of the drug, I was concerned but trusted the professionals. Like the highway shoulder nurses, they kept me talking throughout.

As we landed on the roof of the UC Health Memorial Hospital Central Trauma Center, I was again warned about what was about to happen. "No, thanks, I think I'll bike home," I said.

The next few hours were a battery of seven sequential CT scans, blood tests, dyeing of the internal organs, x-rays, and more. At one point, seeing the many bleeding cuts on my elbows, hands, wrists, knees, hips, ankles, toes, and fingers and feeling the one on the back of my head (notwithstanding the helmet that had cracked in several places), I asked if they were going to do something about them. The attending nurse nonchalantly said, "When we release you, the hospital will take care of those."

What I realized then, which I hadn't known before, was that a trauma center has a binary outcome that determines its professional care success and that is whether you live or die. They are rock stars in the medical profession. They must have the greatest number of saves in the field. My doctor certainly looked the part.

I was released from the trauma center and admitted to the hospital late that afternoon. I survived, yet again. Doctors advised me to go to a rehabilitation center for the next few weeks. I went home.

Several days later was my first foray out of the bed. I went to St. Mary's Church in Aspen, Colorado. I was alone. I prayed. I cried and said aloud "What do you want me to do?"

Life is fragile. Life can end at any given moment. Any. It's humbling. It was the most humbling moment knowing I made more mistakes than deserving of another chance at life. I acknowledge that He had my life at that moment, and He has my life.

June 10, 2019, was the most fortunate day of my life. Not because I survived; rather because I am able to redefine my final moment.

Be deliberate and purposeful in how you live your life.

Live a grateful life. See the beauty in everything.

Live every day knowing one will be your last.

Consider creating your own Code of Conduct.

ABOUT THE AUTHOR

SCOTT FREIDHEIM is a family-focused, community-minded, risk-taking adventurer and businessman.

Scott has experience as a private equity and New York Stock Exchange (NYSE)-traded company CEO and as a board member of for-profit and not-for-profit institutions.

He has served on the most senior leadership teams across multiple industries, including financial services, mass merchandising, brand management, private equity, engineering, and staffing. He has served on the global executive committees of Lehman Brothers (CAO), Investcorp (CEO, Europe), Sears Holdings (EVP and President, Kenmore, Craftsman, and Diehard), and CDI Corporation (Chief Executive Officer). He has run businesses ranging in size from $1 billion to $45 billion.

Scott has served on for-profit boards, including Golden Falcon Acquisition Corp. (Aspen, Colorado), ettain group (Charlotte, North Carolina), N+W Global Vending (Milan, Italy), Icopal (Herlev, Denmark), GL Education (London, England), and Lands' End (Dodgeville, Wisconsin).

He has also served on nonprofit boards, including the US Olympic and Paralympic Committee Foundation (Colorado Springs,

Colorado); Institute of International Education (New York City, New York), which administers the Fulbright Scholarship program; and Spelman College (Atlanta, Georgia).

He is a member of the Economic Club of New York and the Council on Foreign Relations and was named a Young Global Leader by the World Economic Forum. He has participated in many panels at the World Economic Forum in Davos, Switzerland, including as rapporteur for the opening plenary session, as well as at the inaugural New Champions Meeting in Dalian, China. He was also a member of the inaugural World Economic Forum Global Agenda Council.

In 2019, Freidheim was named by *CEO World* as part of Northwestern's #1 ranking in their ranking of universities that produced the greatest CEOs, "Top Universities In The US: Which Produced Greatest CEOs Ever."

Scott is a Knight of the Sovereign Military Order of Saint John of Jerusalem, of Rhodes, and of Malta. He lives in Aspen, Colorado, with his wife, Isabelle, and their three children, Alexander, Leopold, and Anastasia.

E P I L O G U E

WE EACH HAVE THE OPPORTUNITY to create our own Code of Conduct. The good news is that each of us may look into history and decide if we want precedent to serve as a foundation.

In the introduction, I mentioned that my tenets were based on my philosophical and spiritual frameworks. The former is Plato's Cardinal Virtues derived from his book, *The Republic*. Aristotle and other philosophers used them as basis for further teaching. They serve as a comprehensive aspirational framework for life. The framework is meant to capture all virtues in one of the four that are defined.

Throughout this book, I have designated each of my tenets with a symbol to indicate how it fits within Plato's framework. Prudence represented by the owl, Justice represented by the balance, Temperance represented by the lotus flower, and Fortitude represented by the lion. There are eight tenets for each of the four virtues, thus thirty-two in total.

The following is how the tenets in the book fit within the philosophical framework.

Prudence
Reinventing Planning Preparedness Awareness
Strategy Friendships Wisdom Listening

Justice
Gratitude Compassion Equity Ethics Accountability
Transmission Responsibility Communicating

Temperance
Grace Appreciation Humility Love Balance
Prioritize Giving Materialism

Fortitude
Bravery Sustainability Risk Happiness Quo Vadis
Service Relentlessness Faith

On the spiritual front, throughout this book I have designated each tenet with one of eight flags. Each flag represents one of the eight Beatitudes. There are four tenets that relate to each of the Beatitudes, thus thirty-two in total.

Now for a little history and context on the flags. At the Knights of Malta's Chapter General meeting in Montpellier, France, in 1319, it was resolved to group the Knights according to language systems, the so-called Langues or Tongues as opposed to national states. The initial eight were Provence, Auvergne, France, Italy, Aragon, England, Germany, and Castille & Portugal. There is a flag for each.

Today, these flags adorn the Santa Maria church in Aventino at the Magistral Villa of the Sovereign Military Order of Malta (SMOM). The following is how the tenets in the book fit within my spiritual framework.

1. Blessed are the poor in spirit (Provence)
Humility Giving Materialism Service

 2. Blessed are those who mourn (Auverne)
Gratitude Accountability Listening Faith

 3. Blessed are the gentle (France)
Grace Balance Quo Vadis Communicating

 4. Blessed are they who hunger and thirst for uprightness (Italy)
Reinventing Preparedness Transmission Responsibility

 5. Blessed are the merciful (Aragon)
Sustainability Compassion Planning Friendships

 6. Blessed are the pure in heart (England)
Appreciation Ethics Love Happiness

 7. Blessed are the peacemakers (Germany)
Bravery Equity Prioritize Relentlessness

 8. Blessed are those who are persecuted (Castille)
Risk Awareness Strategy Wisdom

Printed in the USA
CPSIA information can be obtained
at www.ICGtesting.com
JSHW021406091223
53550JS00001B/2